THE HOLOCAUST AND GENOCIDE

A Search for Conscience

A Curriculum Guide

by

Richard F. Flaim
and
Edwin W. Reynolds, Jr.
Editors-in-Chief

John Chupak
Harry Furman
Kenneth Tubertini
Contributing Editors

Published by the

Anti-Defamation League of B'nai B'rith

823 United Nations Plaza

New York, N.Y., 10017

<u>Preface</u>

The Holocaust was one of the most shameful episodes in human history. It engulfed not only Jews, but all those unfortunate enough to live under the cloud of Nazi domination. The Jews of Europe, however, were singled out for persecution for one reason: their identity as a people. This then is genocide, the systematic attempt to wipe out an entire people.

The shame of the Holocaust is not unprecedented. There have been mass murders of ethnic groups throughout history. There have been pogroms. There have been massacres in this century, such as the wholesale destruction of the Armenians by the Turks, and there continues today the killing of innocent millions. Never before the Holocaust, however, had the best resources of a state been legally dedicated to mass murder.

Nazi Germany made the destruction of the Jewish people a cornerstone of state policy and power. It built up an elaborate system of death, using its top scientists and its most modern technology to destroy human beings. More than these, however, the Nazi state enrolled its entire civilian population in a conspiracy of silence about the elimination of other civilians, and depended on their cooperation. This is the point of the subtitle: <u>A Search for Conscience.</u>

Perhaps the most important lesson of the Holocaust is that each individual is responsible not only for his or her own actions, but for the consequences which these actions hold for others. The Holocaust was engineered by citizens who were just doing their jobs -- doing them so well that millions of people died. Few of those citizens ever admitted to their individual responsibility for what happened. The Holocaust was only possible because an entire people was condemned by the mere fact of their membership in a group; the victims of the Holocaust were denied their individual identities as precious human beings.

The story of Nazi Germany and its persecution of the Jews and of others whom it would not tolerate is a story of the abdication of individual responsibility and the denial of individual human worth. <u>The Holocaust and Genocide: A Search for Conscience</u> is designed to help students explore the fundamental problem of the individual's relation to the modern state and his or her role in a society of other individuals. This is especially important in a society like our own, which is founded on the rights of the individual and is made up of many different groups.

America is a pluralistic, democratic society. Many ethnic groups, many religious groups, many different individuals, coexist in our country and depend on each other. Without the legal guarantees of individual freedom, upheld by the dictates of each citizen's conscience, peaceful coexistence and toleration might disappear together with the liberty which we so cherish. This is the lesson of <u>The Holocaust and Genocide: A Search for Conscience</u>: that we must accord to every other group or person the same tolerance, recognition and freedom which we seek for ourselves. As Governor of New Jersey, the second most diverse state in the Union, I hope that all New Jerseyans, young and old, will take this lesson to heart.

I have been asked why I feel it important for our children today to study the Holocaust. Why this and not other genocides? Why not forget this painful chapter of history? Why dwell on the evil which man is capable of wreaking on man? My answers to these questions are that it is crucial to remember the events of the Holocaust because it was a uniquely terrible and logical outcome of the creed that one group or person may use force against another with no regard for what is right. It is crucial for this generation and the next to extend its lessons to any incident where the strong exert their wills over the vulnerable. It is crucial not only to recognize that the potential for violence resides in every human being, but also to learn how to prevent violence of any kind against one's fellow humans. We can only do so by remembering the painful lessons of the past and applying them to the future.

Thomas H. Kean
Governor
State of New Jersey

<u>RATIONALE FOR HOLOCAUST AND GENOCIDE STUDIES</u>

Dear Teacher:

I am a survivor of a concentration camp. My eyes
saw what no man should witness:

> Gas chambers built by LEARNED engineers
> Children poisoned by EDUCATED physicians
> Infants killed by TRAINED nurses
> Women and babies shot and burned by HIGH
> SCHOOL and COLLEGE graduates.

So I am suspicious of education.

My request is: Help your students become human.
Your efforts must never produce learned monsters, skilled
psychopaths, educated Eichmanns.

Reading, writing, and arithmetic are important only
if they serve to make our children more humane.

Haim Ginott - <u>Teacher and Child</u>
p. 317

We feel this letter speaks for itself as the rationale for this program.
This curriculum guide represents an attempt to create a program through
which our students will recognize the impact of the inhumanity of human
beings, an impact which comes to ultimately affect their own lives. Study
of the Holocaust and genocide provides countless opportunities to analyze
and discuss some of the most crucial moral and ethical questions which have
faced, and continue to face, the human race. Such issues, if properly treated
in the classroom, must contribute to the moral as well as cognitive development of the students. Hopefully, our students will then become more humane.

The quest for a world society based upon justice and human dignity will
be hindered and delayed until people recognize and move actively to eliminate those factors which create a climate in which genocide in any form can
occur. Knowledge and awareness of those factors will lead to that elimination. The factors are most clearly seen in a study of the Nazi Holocaust.

Unfortunately, there is a general ignorance of the Holocaust in all of
its phases. Traditional treatment of the Holocaust in high school textbooks
has been superficial at best, despite the fact that the Holocaust of 1933-
1945 resulted in the mass murder of millions of people. The results of two

studies were reported in October 1979 at the Second National Conference on Teaching About Genocide and the Holocaust in Secondary Schools, sponsored by the Anti-Defamation League of B'nai B'rith and the National Council of the Social Sciences.

These revealed a serious lack of knowledge on the subject among teachers as well as students, and little emphasis placed upon moral and ethical issues in the schools.

Dr. Glen Pate of the University of Arizona found that among 47 available United States history textbooks, 27 made no mention of the Holocaust or genocide, or at most devoted one line to these topics; only five mentioned the terms specifically; none used both terms; none placed the terms in the index; and median coverage was five sentences.

Princeton University's Dr. Robert Wuthnow conducted a study "What People Know About the Holocaust and Where They Got Their Information." He discovered that of the 1100 respondents, few knew of the Holocaust; those who did received their information from television; all felt "it could happen again" because Americans would obey orders. He urged educators to place more emphasis on historical events and moral values as a way of countering the effects of violence on television and in our society upon our students.

The experiences of the developers of this curriculum guide confirm these findings. We found that students had little or no knowledge of the Holocaust or genocide; students needed improved instruction to facilitate cognitive-moral development, personal decision-making, and to learn the consequences of prejudice and bigotry; and teachers and students needed better curriculum materials. These needs served as motivation for the development of this project.

How is ignorance and superficial treatment of an event so tragic, confounding, and historically recent, possible or tolerated? Young people must understand the Holocaust and the phenomenal impact which that event has had on their world and themselves. They must fully comprehend why such events occur and how they can be prevented. They must fully understand themselves and the significance which issues of conscience and moral judgment must have in their lives.

Elie Wiesel, a Holocaust survivor and novelist, has written: "Perhaps we shall never understand what the Holocaust was, yet this limitation does not free us from the moral responsibility to keep asking questions." Educators must recognize their responsibility to students to provide a much needed background in historical genocide, so that they, in turn, can make rational and moral judgments in determining future directions of our society.

INTRODUCTION

The subject of the Holocaust and genocide is only in its infancy as an
issue for school study. Yet, instructional materials related to the subject
proliferate daily. Educators interested in teaching a unit or course related to the Holocaust and genocide are faced the the difficult task of
selecting those objectives, learning activities and materials which best
meet the needs of their students. This multi-disciplinary curriculum guide
is designed to facilitate this task by providing teachers with a wide
variety of objectives, activities, and materials which have been used success-
fully in a variety of classroom settings. It can be used to develop a
teaching unit or a complete course. It contains activities and materials
which can be incorporated into courses such as psychology, sociology, political
science, history, economics, art, music, philosophy, religion, ethics, and
literature.

This curriculum guide is organized in six units: (1) The Nature of
Human Behavior; (2) Views of Prejudice and Genocide; (3) The Rise of Nazism
in Germany; (4) From Persecution to Mass Murder; (5) Resistance and Intervention; and (6) Related Issues of Conscience and Moral Responsibility.
The units may be taught in sequence as a comprehensive unit of study or course,
or teachers may extract objectives, activities, and materials from any of
the units to supplement their existing programs.

Each unit is preceded by an introduction which provides an overview of
the issue upon which it focuses. Next, a list of each unit's terminal and
performance objectives appears. To facilitate vocabulary development, a
glossary of key words appears in each unit in the section, "Terms." These
terms are defined in a generic sense, as they relate to the Holocaust and
genocide issues treated in the units.

The main portion of the guide consists of a three-columned section. The
left-hand column provides the performance objectives. In the center column,
a diversity of "Learning Activities and Materials" is listed. These activities
and materials are designed to enable the student to achieve the performance
objectives listed in the left-hand column. In an effort to aid the teacher
in the selection of reading materials appropriate to various student reading
levels, each suggested reading is coded as follows:

      BA   -   Below Average Reading Difficulty

      A   -   Average Reading Difficulty

      AA   -   Above Average Reading Difficulty

The determination of the degree of reading difficulty was based upon the
professional judgment of the teachers who have used the materials with high
school students. No readability tests have been used to arrive at these
reading levels. Individual teachers must evaluate the suggested readings in
terms of their own students' reading proficiencies.

While many of the readings included in this guide are suggested for "above average readers," it should be noted that an effort has also been made to include relevant selections from a variety of reading levels. Also, it must be emphasized that many of the learning activities included are applicable to all students. These include the use of discussions, films, debates, moral dilemmas, surveys, simulation games, role playing, values-clarification exercises, poster and painting analyses, poetry and music. The variety is designed to help teachers develop a program of study that is compatible with diverse teaching and learning styles.

Questions relevant to the suggested readings and activities also appear in the center column. An effort was made to include questions from a variety of levels of the cognitive and affective domains. This should facilitate the teacher's task of responding to the diversity of learning styles of students. One should remember that the lists of questions are not all-inclusive, nor are they designed to be used in all situations; teachers are encouraged to select those questions which meet their needs and to add to the lists those which they develop on their own. Additional questions appear in the introductions to readings in The Holocaust and Genocide: A Search for Conscience, An Anthology

All of the materials and activities used in this guide have been field-tested and recommended for use in the classroom. In an effort to assist teachers in the use of these resources, the last column, "Commentary," presents suggestions and practical information which are based upon many years of actual classroom experiences.

An annotated bibliography appears at the back of this guide. It should be useful to teachers in the selection and location of learning materials. Also included are lists of audio-visual distributors, resources and organizations which may be helpful in the planning process.

Finally, the accompanying book, The Holocaust and Genocide: A Search for Conscience, An Anthology consists of a collection of readings and activities which are coordinated with this guide. The anthology is suitable for teacher enrichment as well as use with students.

Because the subject of the Holocaust and genocide is a sensitive issue, teachers must select from the available activities and materials with care and discretion. However, the overwhelming importance of this subject beckons us to treat the issues honestly and squarely.

This guide attempts to improve upon some earlier efforts by providing, as simply as possible, a widespread selection of objectives, activities, materials and suggestions. While it is felt that this guide presents a considerable selection of resources, no document of this nature is ever complete or exhaustive. Thus, teachers are urged to add their own ideas to it and continue to develop Holocaust and genocide-related materials and to share them with their colleagues.

The individuals involved in the development of this document hope that it will contribute to the schools becoming more involved with teaching about Holocaust and genocide and, in the process, develop citizens who respond to moral and ethical issues from a greater sense of conscience.

<u>ACKNOWLEDGEMENTS</u>

<u>THE HOLOCAUST AND GENOCIDE: A SEARCH FOR CONSCIENCE, A CURRICULUM GUIDE</u>
is the result of the efforts of many individuals, agencies, and organizations,
all of whom made important commitments and contributions to its development.
While the specific kinds of contributions varied, all demonstrated a sensitivity
to the needs of students and teachers who must confront the challenge of
learning and teaching about the moral and ethical decisions which resulted
in the Holocaust and other incidents of genocide.

During the spring of 1975, Mrs. Leatrice Rabinsky, a teacher from Cleveland Heights, Ohio, visited the Supervisor of Secondary Social Studies of
the Vineland (NJ) Public Schools to discuss a program in "Literature of the
Holocaust" which she had developed in Ohio. She shared her ideas and materials
and, because of her enthusiasm and success, provided encouragement to Vineland's
staff to pursue curriculum work related to the Holocaust. Mr. Harry Furman,
teacher of social studies at Vineland High School, was authorized to develop
a course of study for an elective course which treated the Holocaust and
related issues of conscience. Coincidentally, in the fall of 1975, the New
Jersey Education Association and the Anti-Defamation League of B'nai B'rith
asked the Vineland and Teaneck school districts to field-test curriculum
materials on the Holocaust developed by Ms. Roselle Chartock and Mr. Jack
Spencer at Monument Mountain Regional High School, Great Barrington, Massachu-
setts. The involvement of Vineland and Teaneck in the field-testing of these
materials served as a catalyst for the extensive efforts by these districts
which has resulted in the creation of this guide and a book of student readings
and activities, <u>THE HOLOCAUST AND GENOCIDE: A SEARCH FOR CONSCIENCE, AN
ANTHOLOGY,</u> (ADL, New York, 1982). The Teaneck Public Schools' prior commitment to Holocaust education involved units within American History II, Modern
European History, and World History courses.

In the fall of 1977, the New Jersey State Department of Education requested
that the Vineland and Teaneck teachers and supervisors, who had developed and
taught units on the Holocaust and genocide, work jointly to develop a teaching
resource guide which could be made available to teachers in the State of New
Jersey. Funds were provided to begin the development of the guide during the
summer of 1978 and the 1978-1979 school year. The first draft of the guide
was presented to the State Department of Education in March, 1979. Important
support and leadership was provided by Dr. Fred Burke, New Jersey Commissioner
of Education, and Deputy Assistant Commissioners Dr. Carl Swanson, and Dr. Paul
Winkler. Dr. Lillian White-Stevens was appointed the State Department of
Education's Holocaust Project Director. She provided invaluable technical
assistance and support throughout the project.

Throughout the six year development of the ideas and materials which are
found in this guide, the Anti-Defamation League of the B'nai B'rith provided
its resources and technical assistance to Vineland and Teaneck. Special appreciation is extended to Ms. Judith Herschlag Muffs of the ADL whose assistance was
invaluable. Among other services, Ms. Muffs, together with Dr. Eleanor Blumen-
berg of ADL, critiqued the first draft of the guide and provided important

suggestions which enhanced its value to educators. Encouragement and support
were provided by Mr. Jeffrey Maas and Ms. Judith Mandelbaum from the New Jersey
ADL. Ms. Ruth Tucker, Librarian at Beth Israel Synagogue, Vineland, New Jersey,
provided expert assistance in locating relevant juvenile literature to be
included in this document. Expert editorial and clerical assistance was provided by Mrs. Betty Castiglia, Mrs. Arleen Flaim, and Mrs. Zitta Reynolds. A
special word of thanks to Theodore Freedman, Director, Intergroup Relations
Division, Anti-Defamation League of B'nai B'rith for his encouragement and
commitment toward the publication of this curriculum.

Appreciation is extended to the Vineland Board of Education and Teaneck
Board of Education and the respective school administrations for their support
and encouragement throughout the development phases of this project. In
addition to their sensitivity to the needs of students and their communities,
they provided the academic freedom to teachers which is crucial to an environment conducive to innovation and experimentation.

The official endorsement of this guide by the New Jersey Council for
the Social Studies is also gratefully acknowledged.

Special appreciation is extended to the teachers who shared their ideas,
feelings, successful classroom experiences, materials and teaching strategies
in an effort to develop a practical guide for their colleagues in the field.
Successful field tests of this guide and accompanying anthology were conducted
in the Vineland and Teaneck schools. In addition to the developers, Mrs. Jeanne
Doremus, Mr. Richard Klimek, and Mrs. Pamela Vander from Vineland High School,
and Dr. Patrick Gallo, Mr. Marc Gruber, Mrs. Berit Heit-Schwarz, Mr. J. Barry
Mascari, Mr. John Mazziotta, and Mr. David Rabadan, from the Teaneck Public
Schools, implemented and evaluated the project's materials.

Finally, special commendations are extended to the contributing editors of
this guide: Mr. Harry Furman from Vineland High School, who provided excellent
leadership to teachers working on various phases of the project, and whose
passion for the subject typifies his work as a teacher; to Mr. Kenneth Tubertini,
also of Vineland High School, who helped to focus attention on the moral and
ethical issues surrounding the Holocaust and related issues of genocide; and to
Teaneck High School's Mr. John Chupak, who made significant contributions to the
variety of non-reading activities found in the guide.

Richard F. Flaim
Social Studies Supervisor
Vineland Public Schools

Edwin W. Reynolds, Jr.
Social Studies Supervisor
Teaneck Public Schools

<u>TABLE OF CONTENTS</u>

UNIT I: THE NATURE OF HUMAN BEHAVIOR

INTRODUCTION

Any study of genocide and the Holocaust must begin with an
overall consideration of the diverse theories of human behavior.
This unit focuses on the potential for good and evil in human
nature. Using the works of literature, philosophy, anthropology,
and sociology by such noted authors as Isaac Bashevis Singer,
Fyodor Dostoevsky, William Golding, Ashley Montagu, Konrad Lorenz,
and many others, the unit probes the capacity of human beings
for aggression, materialism, competitiveness, and ultimately,
murder. Time is spent attempting to define such key concepts as
"rational," "moral," "good," and "evil" which are essential to
such a study. A variety of philosophies of human nature is
reviewed, culminating in students drawing their own preliminary
conclusions about human nature as they progress into subsequent units.
The Kohlberg Scale of Moral Reasoning will be introduced as a means
of comprehending the capacity of individuals for blind partic-
pation in actions which result in suffering.

<u>Unit Goal</u>: There are many theories about human nature and
behavior.

<u>Performance Objectives</u>:

1. The student will recognize that the theme of human nature is
    reflected in literature, music, film, art and personal experience.

2. The student will compare and contrast animal and human behavior.

3. Given anthropological findings, the student will interpret
    human nature.

4. The student will investigate some basic theories of human
    behavior.

5. The student will analyze the role of aggression in Western
    society.

6. The student will analyze the human behaviors of obedience,
    conformity, and silence.

7. The student will draw preliminary conclusions about human behavior.

conscience — The capacity to make decisions based on considerations of justice, universal equity, and moral goodness.

Dani — An Asian island tribe known for its system of ritualized warfare in which human aggression is accepted and brutality in war is sharply limited.

environment — The circumstances, objects, and conditions by which one is surrounded; it is used in this unit to illustrate its effect on individual decision-making.

etiology — The study of animals in their natural habitat.

free will — The power of human beings to make unrestrained choices among alternatives; it is used in this unit to stimulate discussion about the extent to which free will exists in human nature.

Holocaust — The attempted annihilation by the Nazis of European Jews and non-Jews between 1933 and 1945; from the Hebrew word, olah, which means burnt offering.

Ik — An African tribe, studied by anthropologist Colin Turnbull, known for its lack of both family structure and love.

operant conditioning — The process popularized by B. F. Skinner, of obtaining specific behavioral responses by creating an environment which produces positive and negative reinforcement.

rationalism — Reliance upon reason as the basis for truth.

sociobiology — Current school of thought which assumes that human behavior is based upon genetic transmission. Edmund Wilson is a major proponent.

territoriality — The pattern of behavior associated with claiming and defending a specific area.

PERFORMANCE OBJECTIVES	LEARNING ACTIVITIES/MATERIALS	COMMENTARY
		Please note that ANTHOLOGY refers to THE HOLOCAUST AND GENOCIDE: A SEARCH FOR CONSCIENCE: AN ANTHOLOGY FOR STUDENTS.
1. The student will recognize that the theme of human nature is reflected in literature, music, and film.	1. Read from among the following selections which deal with the essence of human behavior.	
	a. "The Grand Inquisitor," The Brothers Karamazov, by Fyodor Dostoevsky, pp. 305-321. AA - Why is the Grand Inquisitor angry with Jesus? - Evaluate Jesus as a character of conscience.	One of the most profound pieces of philosophy in literature, challenging reading, but well worth the time. The brilliant philosophical confrontation between the feared Inquisitor, an aging ruler, and Jesus. Their values clash about freedom, responsibility, and human needs.
	b. "Shiddah and Kuziba," The Spinoza of Market Street, by Isaac Bashevis Singer, pp. 83-88 (See ANTHOLOGY) A - What is ironic about two devils fearing the intrusion of humans? - Are human beings aptly described by Shiddah and Kuziba?	A humorous dialogue between two devils on the dubious nature of humanity.
	c. "Beast from Water," Lord of the Flies, by William Golding, pp. 70-87 A	Shipwrecked English boarding school boys illustrate the nature of "civilized" society and the "beast." Film, "Lord of the Flies," available from Walter Reade.
	d. The Grapes of Wrath, by John Steinbeck, pp. 36-45 (Chapter 5) A - What is the "Monster?"	This selection from the great American Depression novel clearly shows the effect of environment on human behavior.

PERFORMANCE OBJECTIVES	LEARNING ACTIVITIES/MATERIALS	COMMENTARY
	e. The poem, "Adolf Eichmann," _The Essential Lenny Bruce_, John Cohen, ed. (See ANTHOLOGY) A	Eichmann's comparison of the Nazi era with American action in Hiroshima. Provocative.
	- How valid is a comparison of the Holocaust with Hiroshima?	Explores the concept of killing at close range rather than bombing from 40,000 feet. Offers insight into why the Nazis appeared to have difficulty killing Jews at close range.
	f. The poem, "The Unknown Citizen," W. H. Auden A - How does Auden define a "Good Citizen?"	Auden's powerful satirical reaction to the daily life of the "well-adjusted citizen."
	g. "Conversation Concerning Life and Death" from _Marat/Sade_ by Peter Weiss. AA - Compare the ideas of the two characters about life, action, and human behavior.	Notice deSade's harsh attitude toward Nature, and Marat's willingness to act.
	2. Listen to a series of songs about human nature and behavior. Read the lyrics of the songs. Think seriously about the songs and what each says about human behavior. Discuss them and follow up with a broader dialogue on human character and purpose.	Students are not used to _thinking_ about music. Thus, this activity has to be cultivated as a _learning experience_, not simply entertainment. These lyrics should stimulate a passionate discussion about silence, apathy, materialism, the presence of evil, alienation, role-playing, and the meaning of life.
	a. "The Sounds of Silence," by Simon and Garfunkle (See ANTHOLOGY) A - What are the "neon gods?" Does the song describe our own society?	

PERFORMANCE OBJECTIVES	LEARNING ACTIVITIES/MATERIALS	COMMENTARY
	b. "Games People Play," by Joe South - Describe a time when people were "playing games" with you. How would you like people to treat you? c. "The Stranger," by Billy Joel. - How well do you know yourself? Have you ever done something that really surprised you? d. "Sympathy for the Devil," by the Rolling Stones (See ANTHOLOGY) - Is there evil in all of us? e. "Vincent," by Don McLean - Why is Vincent supposedly "too good" for our world? f. "Monster," by Steppenwolf. - What is the Monster? (Relate this to John Steinbeck's monster in The Grapes of Wrath.) g. "Slip Sliding Away," by Paul Simon - How hard do we really try to accomplish our goals? h. "It's Hard to be a Saint in the City," by Bruce Springsteen, - Is it difficult to be "good?" Why? i. "Chimes of Freedom," by Bob Dylan - Who lacks "freedom" in our world? j. "21st Century Schizoid Man" and "Epitaph," by King Crimson (See ANTHOLOGY for "21st Century Schizoid Man") - Are you pessimistic or optimistic about our future?	

PERFORMANCE OBJECTIVES	LEARNING ACTIVITIES/MATERIALS	COMMENTARY

	3. View the cassette-slide program, "An Inquiry into the Nature of Man: His Inhumanity and His Humanity," (Parts I and II) by the Center for the Humanities.
	  - Do people have a natural tendency to commit violence?
	  - Are people more inclined to good or evil?
	  - What is the source of evil?
	
	4. Complete the opinion survey concerning human behavior (See ANTHOLOGY)
	  - Discuss how the responses reflect various viewpoints.
		Beautiful series of paintings and posters which provokes a historical reflection on human potential for good or evil.

2. The student will compare and contrast animal and human behavior.	1. View, "Monkeys, Apes, and Man," and discuss the conclusions suggested by the film.	Students will be particularly fascinated by Harry Haarlow's experiments with baby Rheseus monkeys, and Jane Goodall's work with chimpanzees. The film concludes with a discussion by Desmond Morris which raises arguments about basic human needs and roots, and about the origins of aggression.
	2. Read several of the following selections which compare animal and human behavior: a. "Rats Without Room," Population Control, AEP, pp. 15-19 A - What are the possible implications of these experiments for human behavior and development?	Explanation of the famous Calhoun experiment with rats.
	b. "Fighting," The Naked Ape, by Desmond Morris, pp. 121-131 AA - What is the origin of aggressiveness?	Morris' interpretation of the origin of aggressiveness.

LEARNING ACTIVITIES/MATERIALS

PERFORMANCE OBJECTIVES	LEARNING ACTIVITIES/MATERIALS	COMMENTARY
	c. African Genesis, by Robert Ardrey, pp. 321-345 AA - Explain Ardrey's "Hydraulic Principle."	Makes students aware of the "hydraulic principle," and traditional theories of human aggression.
	d. "Paranoid Hostility," Human Aggression, by Anthony Storr pp. 101-111 AA - Define cruelty. - Are humans more cruel than animals? Why?	Provides an interesting psychological interpretation of why humans are more cruel than animals.
	e. "Man, Aggression, and Men," Men in Groups, by Lionel Tiger and Robin Fox, pp. 199-216 A - Summarize the authors' theory of "Species - specific propensity."	Includes a discussion of Golding's Lord of the Flies, as well as the author's theory of "species - specific propensity" among humans.
	f. "Aggression," Power and Innocence, by Rollo May, pp. 148-161. A - Do you feel that aggression can be constructive and positive? How?	Makes the point that aggression is not always evil and destructive. This piece and the readings below represent a contrast to the previous selections which argue for innate aggressiveness in human beings.
	g. "Humanity's Animal Nature" and "Culture vs Heredity," Could You Kill? - by Alan Jay Fortney, pp. 15-21, 31-37 A - Summarize the author's major thesis in these articles. Do you agree with him? Why?	An excellent summary.
	h. "The Myth of the Beast," The Humanization of Man, by J. Ashley Montagu, pp. 278-83 AA - What is the "Myth of the Beast?"	Montagu brilliantly refutes the idea that humans have learned their aggressiveness from the apes.

PERFORMANCE OBJECTIVES	LEARNING ACTIVITIES/MATERIALS	COMMENTARY
	i. "The Adaptable Primates," _Human Behavior_, by Annette Ehrlich, November, 1976. pp. 25-30. A - Compare Ehrlich's theory with those of Lorenz and Ardrey.	Cogent criticism of Lorenz' and Ardrey's theory that animals are savagely aggressive.
	j. "Is It Our Culture, Not Our Genes, That Makes Us Killers?" _Smithsonian_, by Robert E. Leakey and Roger Lewin, November, 1974, pp. 36-44. AA - React to the environmentalist explanation of human behavior.	Provides the environmentalist explanation of human behavior.
	k. "Who Killed the Guppies?" - (pp. 121-134) "Is Man the Only Immoral Animal?" (pp. 141-144), and "Primitive Tribes" (pp. 152-155) from _Of Animals and Man_, by William Bixby. BA	Excellent readings on aggressive animal and human behavior - man as an immoral animal, and the aggressive Yanamamo tribe of South America.
	3. Read and discuss, "Whispers of Nazi: The Short Political Aberration of Konrad Lorenz," by Richard I. Evans, _Psychology Today_, November, 1974. pp. 84-85. AA	The student should be aware of the congruence between Lorenz' theories and Nazi ideology.
	4. Read and discuss, _Three Faces of Fascism_, by Ernest Nolte, pp. 527-9 AA	Nolte makes the point that Hitler was fascinated with the comparison between human and animal behaviors.
	5. Write an essay in which you compare and contrast opposing viewpoints on animal and human behavior.	
	6. Observe the behavior of animals in a zoo, or of pets at home. Compile a list of the various behaviors. Next to each, note whether there is a parallel behavior in humans.	

PERFORMANCE OBJECTIVES	LEARNING ACTIVITIES/MATERIALS	COMMENTARY
	7. View the film, "The Curious Habits of Man," Discuss the manner in which humans resemble other animals.	
	8. Comment on the following quotation by the 19th-Century German philosopher, Friedrich Nietzsche: "Society has never regarded virtue as anything else than as a means to strength, power and order...there is no such thing as the right to live, the right to work, or the right to be happy...in this respect man is no different from the meanest worm."	Nietzsche sees virtue as an aspect of self interest; examine the comparison of "man" and "worm."
	9. Participate in a debate: "Resolved: Human nature at times defies the laws of nature."	This is an activity to stimulate discussion on the positive and negative aspects of human behavior.
3. Given anthropological findings, the student will evaluate human nature.	1. Read "The Mountain People," by Colin M. Turnbull, _Intellectual Digest,_ April 1973. pp. 49-56. A - How comfortable would you feel living among the Ik? Why?	A selection on the Ik, an African tribe that lives without family structure or love.
	2. View the award-winning film, "Dead Birds." - What does the Dani tribe "say" about warfare and aggression?	An anthropological study of the Dani, a tribe which uses an ancient system of ritualized warfare recognizing, yet contesting, aggression.
	3. Read and discuss, "Learned Aggression," _Could You Kill?_ by Alan Jay Fortney, pp. 23-25, 37, 39. A	
	4. Read chapters 2 and 12, _People of the Lake,_ by Richard E. Leakey and Roger Lewin. - Compare and contrast the authors' view with those of Robert Ardrey.	The authors refute Ardrey by claiming that humans are more sharing and cooperative than aggressive.

PERFORMANCE OBJECTIVES	LEARNING ACTIVITIES/MATERIALS	COMMENTARY
	5. Conduct a critical dialogue examining the possible relationship between the behavior of primitive man and that of individuals in advanced industrial societies. Can primitive humans tell us anything about our behavior and the choices we make in contemporary life?	
	6. Participate in an "Issues and Answers" panel discussion. The panel consists of several "leading anthropologists" who will assess the role of aggression, human defense mechanisms, and peaceful solutions to problems in an ancient human civilization.	
4. The student will investigate some basic theories of human behavior.	1. Read from the following selections which describe additional theories of human behavior. Discuss the theories which are described.	
	a. "Why You Do What You Do, Sociobiology: A New Theory of Behavior," _Time_, August 1, 1977. pp. 54-63 AA	A discussion of a controversial and contemporary school of thought.
	b. "Genes Uber-Alles," _Time,_ December 13, 1976. pp. 93-94 A	Note implication of the "Germanized" title.
	c. "Skinner's Utopia: Panacea, or Path to Hell?" _Time_ September 20, 1971. pp. 47-53 AA	A summary of Skinner's behavioral views.
	d. _Discourse on the Origins of Inequality_, by Jean-Jacques Rousseau, pp. 200-211. AA	The classic Enlightenment view that humans are basically good and are corrupted by society.
	e. _The Anatomy of Human Destructiveness,_ by Erich Fromm. pp. 37-48. AA	Fromm's most recent work; difficult, but provides interesting insights.
	f. "Survival of the Fittest," _On Being Human_, by Ashley Montagu. pp. 15-26. AA	Montagu's attempt to dismiss the theories of the innate destructiveness of humans.

PERFORMANCE OBJECTIVES	LEARNING ACTIVITIES/MATERIALS	COMMENTARY
	2. View the filmstrip, "Free Will and Utopias." Discuss the contrasting theories of free will and determination.	Reviews the basic theories of free will and discusses the Grand Inquisitor.
	3. View the film, "Viva La Liberte." - Why does the man return to his hiding place?	This one-minute allegory depicts the attempt by a man to win his freedom, yet he returns quickly to his hiding place.
	4. Invite theologians of different faiths to express their views of human nature, freedom and free will. Prepare questions to ask these people.	The Protestant, Catholic, and Jewish points of view present interesting contrasts.
	5. Read "The Bus of Quiet Terror," by Stanley L. Englebardt. (See ANTHOLOGY) BA Comment, in writing, on the behavior of the citizens and the deaf students in this account.	This story offers a clear example of positive humanity.
	6. Participate in a "Meeting of the Minds" discussion in which the participants share their views on human nature. Suggested participants could include among others, Charles Darwin, Sigmund Freud, B. F. Skinner, and Karl Marx.	
	7. Construct a magazine article which explains, compares, and contrasts various theories of human nature.	
	8. Participate in the simulation, "Starpower."	This popular simulation can be used as a way to actively show the effects of economic scarcity and the environment on human behavior. It should be presented seriously, but in an atmosphere which will allow students mobility and the chance to express emotions.

STARPOWER - by R. Garry Shirts

Publisher: Western Behavioral Sciences Institute (WBSI)
             1150 Silverado Street, La Jolla, California 92037

Available   Social Studies School Service, 10,000 Culver Boule-
  from: vard, Culver City, California 90230

SIMPLIFIED DIRECTIONS

1. Each student should take 5 chips from the coffee can without
   looking at the can and not showing other people what chips
   he has. He should then quietly compute his present score by
   using the score sheet (either reproduce this on the board or
   give each student a copy).

2. Everyone is told they are going to try to improve their present
   score as much as possible by trading with other people in the
   class. The object of this entire exercise is to get as many
   points accumulated as possible.

3. The trading will occur in the following manner; people will be
   allowed to get up from their seats and move around the room.
   At a given signal, the trading session will begin. Any person
   that is tapped first by an opponent must trade with that
   person. If the tapper gives that person a chip, the opponent
   must exchange chips of a higher value. For example, if I
   tapped someone first and I gave them a blue chip, they must
   return chips worth more than a total of 5 points to me. In
   each case, the tapper gets back more than he gives.

4. The trading session will last 7 minutes during the first round.
   Those persons not wishing to compete may do so but they forfeit
   their chips and accept 50 points as their score.   Everyone
   competing must play the full 7 minute round.

5. When you have completed the trading, write your score and your
   initials under one of the following 3 columns listed on the
   board:

        0-110   111-170   170+

6. Students should separate into those three groups - you have now created a class society.

7. Each group is given three red chips to distribute to its members. These are subsidy chips - each group has two minutes to decide who gets them. Appropriate changes in score should be made.

Round 2

This round should be played exactly like Round 1. Make sure you set the stage by telling everyone you wonder if the lower class, by hard work and effort, will be able to rise to the middle class - and so on. Will the upper class maintain its wealth?

One change: in distributing the chips, the upper class should be given an advantage (more gold and green chips); concurrently, the lower class should be given a can with a preponderance of blue, white, and red chips. Don't tell them this.

Round 2 should be played out to conclusion - examine the changes in alighment in the scoring. At the end of Round 2, those in the upper class may now make the rules for Round 3. They have 3 minutes to make these rules. They can make rules to enhance their position and secure it -- or decide to distribute wealth to others. That is their decision.

Round 3 should be played out. What happens? Does the rest of the group rebel?

All sorts of questions come out of the game related to scarcity, the effects of competition, class structure, the nature of welfare, power, and justice.

PERFORMANCE OBJECTIVES	LEARNING ACTIVITIES/MATERIALS	COMMENTARY

LEARNING ACTIVITIES/MATERIALS

<u>Evaluation Activity</u>

1. Starpower involves a built-in competition to risk in class – How does this affect the people playing the game?

2. Could all members of the class have risen to the upper class in wealth? To the middle class? Why?

3. What was your attitude towards the upper class making the rules for Round 3? If you objected, on what grounds?

4. Were you prepared to rebel against this society? What would you have done? What makes people rebel against a government?

5. How should the rules of the game be made? By one person? By a democratic system? By a republican system?

6. What would have happened if the people elected representatives to make the rules? Why hasn't this happened in the U.S.?

7. Is there anything the people in the bottom class have in common with those above them?

8. Is there any way possible for the upper class to keep its wealth and still have the lower class rise in wealth? If there is, would this keep most of the people from rebelling? If one candidate had made a pledge to do exactly that, would you have voted for him/her?

9. Why doesn't everybody just agree to divide the wealth equally?

<u>Conclusion</u> – Starpower is concerned with three essential problems of life: dividing up the wealth, deciding who will make rules(laws) and considering why people rebel or don't rebel against a particular power.

Remember that list of "things" essential to your happiness. At what point would you be prepared to rebel against any powerful force that tried to deprive you of those "things?" In other words, what has to happen in a society to you <u>or</u> to someone else for you to stand up in opposition?

PERFORMANCE OBJECTIVES	LEARNING ACTIVITIES/MATERIALS	COMMENTARY
5. The student will analyze the role of aggression in Western society.		Although the major focus of the activities for performance objective 5 is on sports, alternative activities from business, politics, crime, etc., may be used.
	1. View and react to the film, "Violence Just For Fun." - How do you explain the spectator response to gladiatorial combat?	Depicts gladiator combat and spectator response.
	2. View the film, "Corrida Interdite." - Why are violent sports so popular?	Silently pieces together the process of the bullfight.
	3. Read and discuss the following selections: a. "Coliseum and Gladiators" and "Cultural Revolution: Socialism and Fascism" in Rip-Off: The Big Game, by Paul Hoch, pp. 16-25, 190-195. A	A critical analysis of the functions and future of sport in American society.
	b. "The Giant in the Tube," by Anton Myrer, Harper's, November, 1972, pp. 40-56. A	A comparison of football and baseball, explaining why the former better suits America; also deals with the violent language of sports.
	c. Out Of Their League, by Dave Meggysey, pp. 46-48, 144-147. A - How does football resemble the military?	Written by an ex-professional, this is one of the first books critical of football. The selection highlights the philosophy of the game and the response of professional football to the assassination of President Kennedy in 1963.

PERFORMANCE OBJECTIVES	LEARNING ACTIVITIES/MATERIALS	COMMENTARY
	4. Play the song, "Hometeam Crowd," by Louden Wainwright and discuss what it means to be a spectator.	
	5. Play "Who Killed Davey Moore?" by Bob Dylan. - What is the message of this song?	
	6. Write a research paper or an essay in which you compare the role of aggression in Eskimo or Tasaday society with that of the United States.	
6. The student will analyze the human behaviors of obedience, conformity, and silence.	1. Read "The Dying Girl That No One Helped," by Loudon Wainwright. (See ANTHOLOGY) BA	The comments of some of the spectators who watched Kitty Genovese die should elicit responses.
	2. Read "The Milgram 'Shock' Experiment." (See ANTHOLOGY) A OR View the film, "Moral Development." - What did Milgram's experiment prove?	A dramatization of the famous Stanley Milgram shock experiments which were originally developed to compare American and German capacity to commit violence on perfect strangers. The film explains the Lawrence Kohlberg Theory of the six stages of moral development.
	3. Read "You Will Do As Directed," by Ron Jones (See ANTHOLOGY) A - Why were the students willing to follow Jones even beyond the point at which he was satisfied? - Do you feel students are more likely to reject or accept such authority? Why?	"The Wave" is an excellent television dramatization of this experience.

<table>
<tr><td>PERFORMANCE OBJECTIVES</td><td>LEARNING ACTIVITIES/MATERIALS</td><td>COMMENTARY</td></tr>
<tr><td>7. The student will draw preliminary conclusions about human behavior.</td><td>

1. Debate, "Resolved: Human beings are innately aggressive and warlike."

2. Write an essay in which you summarize your views about human nature and behavior. Focus specifically on the human capacity for good or evil and the ability to handle freedom, responsibility, truth, pain, etc.

3. In small groups, discuss the meaning of the following quotation by Karl Marx, and present your group conclusions to the class:

"It is not the consciousness of men that determines their existence, but on the contrary, their social existence that determines their consciousness."

4. Holocaust victim Anne Frank once said, " In spite of everything, I still believe that people are really good at heart."

   - How do you react to her view?

5. Write an essay in which you examine the following quotation from Oscar Wilde:

"For each man kills the thing he loves
By each let this be heard
Some do it with a bitter look
Some with a flattering word
The coward does it with a kiss
The brave man with a sword."

</td><td>

It is suggested that the teacher ask students to write their preliminary generalizations about human behavior at l the conclusion of this unit. These should be held by the students or the teacher as succeeding units to review their conclusions.

</td></tr>
</table>

LEARNING ACTIVITIES/MATERIALS

6. Prepare a bulletin board which presents various views of human nature.

7. Construct a work of art, either a painting, sculpture, or a collage, which symbolizes student conclusions about human character.

8. In Charlie Chaplin's "Monsieur Verdoux," Chaplin plays a little bank clerk who, anxious to provide for his family, shifts to the career of a professional bluebeard, marrying wealthy women and then doing away with them. He finds a young girl just released from jail, lonely, desperate, starving and abandoned in the street. He takes her up to his "study," treats her to breakfast and brings in two glasses of wine, one of them containing poison. She tells him a story of the mess and misery into which she was drawn by her love. He exchanges her glass for one without poison. Afterward, when he urges her to leave much against her will, but provided with money and good wishes, he pushes her out, imploring "Go away! You have corrupted my morals."

What does Monsieur Verdoux mean by "morals?" Is there such a thing as absolute morality? Of what does it consist? Are there any human responsibilities you feel you have?

9. Conduct the following experiments involving individual capacity for involvement:

a. The experiment will require at least three students. One will observe and record. Two students will walk down a busy sidewalk, one of them holding a can of soda. Just as they are about to pass another person coming in the opposite direction, the student should throw the can onto the sidewalk. A trash can should be clearly visible only several steps away. What will the passerby do?

Activities 6 and 7 might appeal to all students, but especially to the artistically gifted and talented.

PERFORMANCE OBJECTIVES	LEARNING ACTIVITIES/MATERIALS	COMMENTARY

(1) Nothing, simply ignore the circumstance and go on.

(2) Exhibit some sort of body language which indicates distaste for what has happened, but nothing else.

(3) Quietly pick up the can and discard it in the trash.

(4) Directly confront the student and request that he/she pick up the can and discard it.

Record the results. Make sure you have an adequate sample to draw conclusions. Wait a sufficient period of time so that the next passersby have not seen what has transpired.

Now change some of the control factors:

1. Increase the <u>numbers</u> in the group walking. Will this lessen the degree of involvement?

2. Change the <u>racial</u> composition of the students. Will there be less confrontation of certain groups?

3. Change the <u>gender</u> of the students. Does this affect the results?

4. Change the <u>location</u> to the school parking lot where students are dealing with their peers. Any change?

Draw conclusions about the human capacity for involvement in this very simple circumstance. Interview some of the citizens involved in the experiment. Can you draw a profile of the persons who will or will not become involved?

b. Select one other student and participate in the following experiment with the cooperation of your teacher.

The teacher should leave a watch on the desk in the classroom and come to class about one minute late. Several
minutes before the bell, a student (who has been previously
informed) should come into the room, hang around the desk,
and then overtly take the watch and go to his/her seat.
The student should boast to some classmates that he or she
is going to "pull one over on the teacher." The teacher
should come into the room and begin the lesson. Later,
the teacher should notice the watch is gone, look around,
and ask the class if anyone knows what happened to it.

Note the individual and group reactions to the teacher's
question. Continue to note reactions when and if the
teacher resumes the lesson.

The next day, inform your classmates about the experiment
which you and the teacher conducted. Lead a discussion
assessing the varied reactions.

- Why were students willing/unwilling to report the offender?
- What would be the implications to society if everyone
  behaved as you did?

- What conclusions can be drawn from this experiment?

10. Read "The Mayor's Choice: What would you do?" (See ANTHOLOGY)

-Respond to the questions.

-Compare your responses in class discussion.

The focus of this discussion
should be on the moral issues
involved in making choices in
situations where right and wrong
behavior is not well defined
by society.

UNIT II: VIEWS OF PREJUDICE AND GENOCIDE

INTRODUCTION

This unit encourages the student to probe the concept of
genocide, the systematic murder of people sharing common
characteristics. Particular emphasis is placed upon the causes
and origins of prejudice, and the nature of stereotyping and
scapegoating. Emphasis is also placed on historical examples
of genocide, including the destruction of the Armenians early
in this century and the plight of the contemporary "boat people."
The student should examine his/her own capacity for pre-judgment
and its consequences.

<u>Unit Goal</u>: Historical incidents have demonstrated that genocide
maybe the outcome of applied prejudice, scapegoating and discrimination.

<u>Performance Objectives</u>:

1. The student will determine the basic causes of prejudice,
    scapegoating and discrimination.

2. The student will examine the history of anti-Semitism
    before 1933.

3. The student will define the concept of genocide.

4. The student will reassess his/her generalizations about
    human nature inlight of historical incidents of genocide.

TERMS

Armenia	A former kingdom of Northeast Asia Minor, including Eastern Turkey. In the late 1800's and early part of this century the Armenians were victims of genocide at the hands of the Turks.
assimilation	The act of becoming part of a large culture by absorbing its values as one's own.
dehumanization	Divesting of human qualities or personality.
ethnocentrism	The tendency for people to feel that their race, religion, culture, or nation is superior.
genocide	The use of deliberate systematic measures calculated to bring about the murder of an entire racial, political or cultural group.
nativism	An attitude or policy favoring the native inhabitants of a country over immigrants.
scapegoat	A person, group, or object given blame for the mistakes or failures of others.
stereotype	A generalized image of a person or group; the characteristics seen in a few are ascribed to the whole.

PERFORMANCE OBJECTIVES	LEARNING ACTIVITIES/MATERIALS	COMMENTARY
		Please note that ANTHOLOGY refers to THE HOLOCAUST AND GENOCIDE: A SEARCH FOR CONSCIENCE: AN ANTHOLOGY FOR STUDENTS.
1. The student will evaluate the basic causes of prejudice, scapegoating and discrimination.	1. Participate in the activity, "Attitudes Toward Groups." (See ANTHOLOGY)	
	2. Read from among the following selections; discuss what each selection "says" about prejudice.	
	a. "I Ain't Sleepin Nexta No Nigger," in _Prejudice and Discrimination_, edited by Jack Fraenkel, pp. 23-25. (See ANTHOLOGY) BA	Describes Sammy Davis, Jr.'s first encounter with racism in the army.
	b. _The Nature of Prejudice_, by Gordon Allport, pp. 325-333. AA	Allport offers the basic frustration concept of prejudice; the place to start in any discussion of the roots of prejudice, frustration, aggression, and displacement.
	c. _The ABC's of Scapegoating_, by Gordon Allport. A	
	d. Ecidujerp, _Prejudice_, by Irene Gersten and Betsy Bliss, pp. 20-27 (See ANTHOLOGY) BA – What can motivate prejudice?	
	e. _The Painted Bird_, by Jerzy Kosinski, pp. 43-54 (See ANTHOLOGY) A	This is a story of how color, even "beautiful" color can cause prejudice and death.
	f. _White Over Black_, by Winthrop Jordan AA "The Blackness Without," pp. 4-11 "The Evaluation of Color," pp. 252-259 "The Disease of Color," pp. 517-521	The classic study that links the impact of color and religious doctrines to racism.

PERFORMANCE OBJECTIVES	LEARNING ACTIVITIES/MATERIALS	COMMENTARY
	g. <u>Women in a Sexist Society</u>, by Vivian Gornick and Barbara Moran: AA "Working in a Man's World," by Roslyn Willett, pp. 511-532 "Thy Neighbor's Wife, Thy Neighbor's Servants," by Catherine Stimpson, pp. 622-658	This work deals with the issues of sex as a motivation for prejudice and discrimination.
	h. "The Motive to Avoid Success," in <u>The American Woman</u>, pp. 41-48 A	Describes several examples which display the negative effects of social values on women's growth.
	3. Listen to the song, "Woman is the Nigger of the World," by John Lennon and Yoko Ono. - Explain what this song means to you.	This song from the album, "Shaved Fish," is a condemnation of the treatment of women in today's society.
	4. View and react to the following audio-visual materials:	
	a. "The Prejudice Film" (Film)	David Hartman narrates this review of the different stages of prejudice, discrimination, and scapegoating.
	b. "Seeds of Hate" (Filmstrip)	A basic study of the causes of prejudice; good for a knowledge of the vocabulary of prejudice.
	c. "Stereotyping, Part I" (Filmstrip)	Relates stereotyping to prejudice and differentiates it from "valid generalizations."
	d. "The Victims" (Film)	Dr. Benjamin Spock discusses the causes of prejudice in children.
	e. "You've Got To Be Taught To Hate" (Film)	Shorter version of "The Victims."

PERFORMANCE OBJECTIVES	LEARNING ACTIVITIES/MATERIALS	COMMENTARY
	e. "The Distorted Image" (Slide Presentation)	Depicts the image of various immigrant groups in 19th and 20th century newspapers and magazines.
	5. Play the song, "Word Game" by Stephen Stills (See ANTHOLOGY) - Debate the accusations of Stills.	Deals with the way people treat each other.
	6. Analyze how a racial or ethnic group has been stereotyped by the media. Select any racial or ethnic group and prepare a log in which you record examples of media stereotyping. - What conclusions can you draw?	
	7. Complete the following statements: a. All fat people are _________________. b. Blondes have more _________________. c. People on welfare are _________________. d. Jews are _________________. e. Black people with "Afros" are _________________. f. Chinese are _________________. g. All teachers are _________________. h. White people are _________________. i. All Indians are _________________. j. All Hispanics are _________________. After you have completed the sentences, join a small group in which you compile a list of the adjectives used by the group members to complete the statements. - Is there a pattern in the responses which are listed? How do you explain the pattern? - Eased upon what you know, how do we acquire stereotypes?	

	8. Read the selections dealing with stereotypes in Gordon Allport's THE NATURE OF PREJUDICE. What additional insight does the reading provide in relation to the hypothesis you developed in answering the question above?	
	9. Read "A Hatemonger Sells Himself to Michigan." (See ANTHOLOGY) A - Why do you think he was nominated? - Why do you think groups such as the Ku Klux Klan and the Neo-Nazis continue to attract members?	The article is about the nomination for Congress of Gerald Carlson for Michigan. He is a white supremacist and former Nazi.
	10. Propaganda is a clever device used to develop and manipulate prejudice. It was crucial to the development of Nazism. Read "Propaganda Posters and Leaflets." (See ANTHOLOGY) A - Analyze the appeals made in current American right-wing propaganda - How are various ethnic groups portrayed? What is the basic appeal? - How does this propaganda exhibit the concept of ethnocentrism? - Do you feel pamphlets such as these should be banned from circulation in the United States? Explain your point of view.	
	11. Prepare a collage, scrapbook, painting, or slogan which illustrates the concept of prejudice. Fully explain how your artistic effort demonstrates the concept	
2. The student will examine the history of anti-Semitism before 1933.	1. Read "Not Citizens Only Subjects," in Never to Forget, by Milton Meltzer, pp. 3-9, and "The City of Slaughter," in The World of Our Fathers: The Jews of Eastern Europe, by the same author, pp. 185-189. BA - How has the response to Jews evolved since the birth of Jesus? - What is a pogrom? What does "The City of Slaughter" tell you about anti-Semitism outside of Germany?	

PERFORMANCE OBJECTIVES	LEARNING ACTIVITIES/MATERIALS	COMMENTARY
	2. Read "Jewish Life In Europe: Between the Two World Wars," in _The Holocaust Years: Society on Trial_, edited by Chartock and Spencer, pp. 67-78 A - React to what you have read.	
	3. Read "The Character of the Jew," in _What It Means To Be A Jew_, by Charles Shulman, pp. 32-40. AA - Summarize the "Jewish character."	
	4. Read "I Was, With God's Help, a Poor Man," in _World of Our Fathers: The Jews of Eastern Europe_, by Milton Meltzer, pp. 66-73. A - Describe life in the shtetl.	
	5. Construct a chart in which you compare and contrast the beliefs and customs of Judaism and Christianity.	
	6. Participate in a "What I Know About Christians and Jews" activity, in which Christian students discuss what they know about Judaism; and Jewish students discuss what they know about Christianity. - What conclusions can you draw from this activity?	
	7. View the feature film, "Lies My Father Told Me" (Columbia, 102 min., color).	Jan Kadar's moving evocation of life in Montreal's Jewish ghetto. A young boy clings to his grandfather during his parent's turmoils. Describes the differing values of the assimilated and non-assimilated Jew.
	8. Read _The Fixer_, by Bernard Malamud, pp. 109-115. A - Do you think The Fixer was judged guilty before the trial? Why?	A moving account of a young Jew in Russia accused of a ritual murder, and his attempt to survive in the face of vicious anti-Semitism.

PERFORMANCE OBJECTIVES	LEARNING ACTIVITIES/MATERIALS	COMMENTARY
	9. Read "Religious and Racial Anti-Semitism." (See ANTHOLOGY) BA - How do you respond to the charge that organized Christianity might have had a large role in the historic treatment of Jews?	Provides a basic overview of Jewish-Christian relations since the time of Jesus.
	Respond to the dilmemma, "Conversion or Emigration?" (See ANTHOLOGY).	
3. The student will define the concept of genocide.	1. In small groups, discuss the validity of the following statements: a. "Genocide can never be eliminated because it is deeply rooted in human nature." b. "Given certain economic conditions, any group can become the victim of **genocide.**" NOT? c. "Historically, those in power use genocide to retain power." d. "Given certain social and political conditions in the United States, an unassimilated racial or ethnic group could become the victims of genocide."	
	2. Read "Cain and Abel, The First Genocide," in _Messengers of God._ by Elie Wiesel, pp. 50-75 AA - Discuss the implications of what you have read.	A fascinating interpretation of the first murder and the roles of Cain, Abel, and God.
	3. Prepare an article for your local newspaper on the topic, "Why Genocide?" In your article, analyze the causes of genocide.	
	4. View the film, "The Lottery," or read the short story in _Points of View, An Anthology of Short Stories_, edited by Agnes Moffett and Kenneth R. McElheny, pp. 556-565. A - What are the implications of this film or story?	Portrays the systematic murder of one member of a community each year.

PERFORMANCE OBJECTIVES	LEARNING ACTIVITIES/MATERIALS	COMMENTARY
	5. Write letters to the United Nations, the American Government, and a selected foreign country in which you ask each for an official definition of genocide, a position on it, and an explanation of actions they would suggest in dealing with the crime. —Compare and contrast your findings.	
4. The student will reassess his/her generalizations about human nature in light of histor-ical inicidents of Genocide.	1. Read each of the selections below: a. Passage to Ararat, by Michael Arlen, pp. 25-136, 151-184, 202-240, 241-250. (See ANTHOLOGY)	Arlen explains some basic Armenian history and draws some comparisons between the Armenian and Jewish genocides.
	b. Forty Days of Musa-Dagh, by Franz Werfel AA	Classic novel about the Armenian massacre.
	c. The Smyrna Affair, by Marjorie Housepian, pp. 116-121, 141-154, 198-211. A - Why did the Ottoman Government use the Armenians as scapegoats? - How do you think the United States should have responded to the Armenian genocide?	Graphically describes the horrors of the massacre by the Turks in the city of Smyrna in 1922.
	2. Prepare an outline in which you trace the history of the Armenian genocide. Include in your outline significant events, personalities and dates.	
	3. Construct a chart in which you compare the Armenian genocide with the Holocaust.	
	4. Read "The Forgotten Genocide" (See ANTHOLOGY) A/BA - What impact might this genocide have had on the rise of Adolf Hitler?	Includes excerpts from Passage to Ararat, by Michael Arlen, and Some of Us Survived, by Kerop Bedoukian, who vividly recalls his childhood experiences. Simply written.

PERFORMANCE OBJECTIVES	LEARNING ACTIVITIES/MATERIALS	COMMENTARY

5. Apply the diagram, "Steps of Organized Genocide," to Armenian history.

      Denial of Justice
      ↓
      Isolation
      ↓
      Propaganda
      ↓
      Persecution

Dehumanization   Violence   →   Execution

6. In a small or large group, discuss the following statement in relation to the Armenian genocide:

"History has little space for lost causes, no patience for losers, no time for the powerless and no tolerance for the weak."

7. Comment on the statement made by Adolf Hitler on the use of his genocide policy?

"Who still tells nowadays of the extermination of the Armenians?"

8. View and discuss the film, "The Armenian Case," or the abridged version, "The Forgotten Genocide."

9. Read "Slaughter of the Innocents," in _Newsweek_, July 2, 1973.
   - React to the genocide in Burundi.   A

10. Read "Agony of the Boatpeople," in _Newsweek_, July 2, 1979. A
    - How do you feel about the plight of the boatpeople?

11. Read "The Moral Problem of Refugees," in _New Republic_, by Michael Walzer, February 10, 1979, pp. 15-17.   AA
    - Does the United States have any moral responsibility toward these people?

12. Read and discuss "Biafra, the End," and "Accomplices," from
    <u>A New Today</u> by Eli Wiesel, pp. 29-31. (See ANTHOLOGY) A

13. Compare and contrast the experiences of the Armenians, the
    Boatpeople, and the Cambodians in relation to genocide.

14. Listen to the song, "Bangladesh," by George Harrison.
    - How do you react to what Harrison is saying?

15. Apply the diagram, "Steps of Organized Genocide," to one of
    the following groups:

    a. American Indians
    b. Chinese
    c. Japanese
    d. Polish
    e. Irish
    f. Russians
    g. English
    h. Christians
    i. Moslems
    j. Buddhists
    k. Haitians
    i. Hispanics

    - Has the group you selected been a victim of genocide?

16. Read and discuss, "How were the Indian Tribes Destroyed?"
    (See ANTHOLOGY) A

17. Read "Cambodian Genocide." (See ANTHOLOGY) A
    - Who is responsible for this genocide?
    - How has the world reacted to this example of genocide?

18. Respond to "The Councilperson's Dilemma." (See ANTHOLOGY) A

PERFORMANCE OBJECTIVES	LEARNING ACTIVITIES/MATERIALS	COMMENTARY
	19. Listen to the song, "Driven to Tears," by The Police. (See ANTHOLOGY) - What does this song say about the reality of the Cambodian genocide? - How do you feel about what you have heard? 20. Listen to a recording of "Waiting for the Worms," by Pink Floyd (See ANTHOLOGY) - Fully explain the meaning of the lyrics to this song. 21. Read "The Passion of Mrs. Wiget," (See ANTHOLOGY) A - How do you feel about this woman's response to the plight of the "boatpeople?"	The use of music which is popular among students can be an excellent learning activity. It has been found that, while students are familiar with the melody, they often do not analyze the lyrics for meaning. The selections suggested in 19 and 20 deal with the "Cambodian Genocide" and imminent genocide, respectively.

UNIT III: THE RISE OF NAZISM IN GERMANY TO 1933

INTRODUCTION

In this unit, the student will investigate the various
reasons for the rise of the Nazi Party, its ideology in Germany.
Considering economic, sociological, and psychological explana-
tions, the student will explore the basic values inherent in
Nazism. He/she will attempt to explain the rise of anti-
Semitism as well as the concepts of nationalism, totalitarianism,
and the authoritarian personality.

<u>Unit Goal</u>:   A variety of global and domestic conditions led
to the emergence of the Nazi Party and its ideology in Germany.

<u>Performance Objectives</u>:

1.   The student will explain Germany's rise to power in the
     19th and 20th centuries.

2.   The student will assess the influence of the Versailles
     Treaty upon the rise of Adolf Hitler and the Nazi Party.

3.   The student will investigate the reasons for the decline
     of the Weimar Republic.

4.   The student will examine the broad appeal of Nazi philosophy
     and government.

5.   The student will state and support generalizations about the
     reasons for the rise of the Nazi state.

anti-Semitism — Hostility towards Jews.

Aryan — In Nazi ideology, a Nordic-type Caucasian Gentile.

authoritarian personality — A concept developed by Theodore Adorno which identifies the characteristics of those individuals who are most easily swayed by demagogic appeals.

blood purity — The "undiluted" nature of Teutonic blood.

Bismarck, Otto Von — The Prussian "Iron Chancellor" who unified Germany in the late 19th century.

demagogue — A person who influences others by appealing to emotion and prejudice.

Der Stuermer — A racist, hate-filled, government-sponsored newspaper, edited by Julius Streicher, and popular with the Nazis.

dolchstoss — A popular theme of the Nazi Party, suggesting that Germany had been "sold out" by Jews and others in World War I; Literally means, "stab in the back."

Eichmann, Adolf — The man who, working closely with Heinrich Himmler, was responsible for implementation of the "Final Solution."

eugenics — The study of human improvement by genetic control.

fascism — A system of government characterized by a dictatorship of the extreme right, a merging of state and business leadership, and a belligerent nationalism.

Free Corps — A paramilitary group of World War II officers and veterans who opposed the Weimar Republic and contributed to the rise of the Nazi Party.

Gestapo — The German Secret Police created in 1933 to eliminate political opposition.

Goebbels, Joseph — The Minister of Propaganda under Hitler.

Goering, Hermann — The second ranking Nazi and the field marshall responsible for the operation of the Luftwaffe.

Himmler, Heinrich — The Reichsfuehrer who developed and led the SS.

Hindenburg, Otto Von — The World War I hero and President of Germany under the Weimar Republic, who turned over the Chancellorship to Adolf Hitler in 1933.

Junkers

The German aristocratic landowners; this "old guard" conservative group has been accused of helping Hitler rise to power.

Kaiser

The title of the ruler of Germany (1871-1918).

Kohlberg Scale

The six stage scale created by Dr. Lawrence Kohlberg to identify the levels of moral reasoning.

Lebensborn

The eugenics program instituted by the Nazis to perfect the German "race."

Luftwaffe

The German Air Force.

mysticism

A spiritual discipline by which one attempts to unite with the divine through deep meditation or contemplation.

narcissim

The excessive admiration of self.

Oedipus complex

The libidinal feelings of a male child for his mother, accompanied by hostility to his father; used in this unit to refer to Hitler's feelings towards his parents.

Pogrom

An organized massacre of a minority group, term first used in regard to Jews in Eastern Europe. Derived from the Russian word meaning "like thunder; devastation."

Protocols of the Elders of Zion

A false account depicting the supposed take-over of the world by Jewish leaders and businessmen.

psychoanalysis

The analytic technique developed by Sigmund Freud to investigate and treat mental disorders.

psychopath

A personality disorder in which one often manifests aggressively anti-social behavior.

Prussia

A former kingdom and state in Germany which was noted for its military power.

putsch

A sudden attempt by a group to overthrow a government; used in this unit to refer to the unsuccessful Munich Putsch of Adolf Hitler in 1923.

Reichstag

The German legislature.

reparations

The money and goods paid by Germany to the Allies after World War I.

SS   The universal abbreviation for Schutzstaffel, the
                        Elite Guard. Served as political police and were
                        responsible for destroying the Jews in Europe.

Versailles Treaty   The punitive Peace Treaty signed after World War I,
                        which established the system of reparations and
                        blamed the war on Germany.

Volk   The mystical German concept of "the people," claiming
                        that all Aryans innately carry the same spirit.

Weimar Republic   Germany's experiment with republican government which
                        grappled with post-war guilt, inflation, and severe
                        right-wing opposition, until its fall in 1933.

UNIT III – Unit Goal   A variety of global and domestic conditions led to the emergence of the Nazi
                Party and its ideology in Germany.

PERFORMANCE OBJECTIVES	LEARNING ACTIVITIES/MATERIALS	COMMENTARY
1. The student will explain Germany's rise to power in the 19th and 20th centuries.	1. View one or more of the following films and/or filmstrips. Summarize the main themes and write out any questions you have regarding the subject matter. Answer your questions as you move through the unit. a. "From Kaiser to Fuhrer" b. "The Making of the German Nation" c. "The Twisted Cross" d. "Mein Kampf" e. "The Rise and Fall of Adolf Hitler" (four part filmstrip) 2. Read the following selections from the Xerox publication, Nazi Germany. A Develop questions related to your reading and discuss the answers to those questions with others in the class. "From Hope to Despair," pp. 1-4 "Ernst Tollar's Experience," pp. 5-11 "The Weimar Republic," pp. 13-21 (See ANTHOLOGY) "Halberg Goes Nazi," pp. 27-45 "Hitler Becomes Fuhrer," pp. 47-52. 3. Construct a chart in which you show the different interpretations for the rise of the Nazi State as indicated in John Snell's, The Nazi Revolution. AA 4. Participate in one of the following debates about the rise of the Nazis. - Adolf Hitler's presence guaranteed the victory of the Nazi Party. - European power politics strongly influenced the rise of the Nazis.	Please note that ANTHOLOGY refers to THE HOLOCAUST AND GENOCIDE: A SEARCH FOR CONSCIENCE: AN ANTHOLOGY, FOR STUDENTS. Historic films which catalog Hitler's move from obscurity to the Chancellorship of Germany. A series of readings which offers the traditional interpretation for the rise of Nazism. "Weimar" provides a basic historical background to the post-war years.

PERFORMANCE OBJECTIVES	LEARNING ACTIVITIES/MATERIALS	COMMENTARY
	- Nazism was an outgrowth of German history. - Nazism was a national uprising against non-German postwar forces. - Nazism was largely a result of the crisis of capitalism. - Nazism was a product of the promise and failure of socialism. - Nazism was security for the "sick psyche" of the German people. 5. Present to a large group the various historical interpretations for the rise of Nazism. In a brainstorm, rank these interpretations in order of importance. Justify the ranking. 6. Construct a chart in which you trace the spread of militarism, nationalism, and imperialism in Germany during the years 1870-1938. Your chart should be divided into three sections corresponding to these concepts. There should be appropriate space allotted to historic examples and a brief description should be included. 7. Read All Quiet on the Western Front by Erich Maria Remarque, pp. 133-140. A - How do you think this kind of experience affected the future decisions of individuals? 8. Construct an underground newspaper which reflects what might have been done to stop the rise of Nazism. 9. Construct a bulletin board display, collage, or poster exhibition which illustrates the factors which contributed most to Hitler's rise to power.	A devastating account of the horror and inhumanity of World War I from the perspective of a German soldier. The film based on the book is also available.

10. Read the following poems:

"Father in Heaven, resolved to the death
Kneel we before Thee, Oh answer us, then!
Does ought other people Thine awful command
More loyalty follow than we Germans do?

Is there one such? The Eternal One, send
Laurel and victory to it, mighty with Fate
Father, Thou smilest? Oh, joy without end!
Up! and onward, onward to the holy crusade."
                                    - Dietrich Eckart

"Color all the pastures, all the stalls
White with their bones
Those which the raven and the fox disdain
Deliver them over to the fish,
Damn up the Rhine with their corpses...

"Silent night! Holy Night!
All is calm, All is bright
Only the Chancellor steadfast in fight
Watches o'er Germany by day and by night
Always caring for us.

"Silent night! Holy night!
All is calm, All is bright."

- What do these selections mean to you?

PERFORMANCE OBJECTIVES	LEARNING ACTIVITIES/MATERIALS	COMMENTARY
2. The student will assess the influence of the Versailles Treaty upon the rise of Adolf Hitler and the Nazi Party.	1. Describe Hitler's appeal to the following individuals in Germany. Use the Versailles Treaty as your point of reference: a. an unemployed shipbuilder b. a miner c. a career army officer d. a factory worker involved with the labor movement e. a junker f. a young teenager g. a housewife in East Prussia. - Can you assume an individual's political views from his/her economic interests? Why? 2. Participate in a debate on the following proposition: "Resolved: The Treaty of Versailles Doomed the Weimar Republic." 3. Construct a German newspaper dated 1932, in which you appraise the impact of the Versailles Peace settlement upon German civilians. Include editorials, advertisements, political appeals of the time, and major events. 4. Assume the role of a leader of the Weimar Republic and participate in an "Issues and Answers" program in which you defend your government's programs. The questions you answer should represent the various attitudes towards the Republic. 5. The Free Corps, a group of disgruntled German war veterans who would ultimately join with the Nazis, composed the following: "Come on boys, let's all go... Off to the pogrom with a ho, ho, ho. Put in your bellies and throw out the Jews With swastika and poison gas Let's have a go at murder in the mass." - What is the irony of this poem written 14 years before Hitler's rise to power?	

PERFORMANCE OBJECTIVES	LEARNING ACTIVITIES/MATERIALS	COMMENTARY
	6. Participate in a mock trial in which German attorneys challenged the validity of Article 231 in an international court.	An activity which enables students to examine both sides of the Versailles Treaty. Witnesses should explore the roles played by the various countries in the war; imperialism alliances, and militarism as factors causing World War I; and the impact of the Treaty upon Germany.

PERFORMANCE OBJECTIVES	LEARNING ACTIVITIES/MATERIALS	COMMENTARY

3. The student will investigate the reasons for the decline of the Weimar Republic.	1. List the positive and negative aspects of the Weimar Republic. Discuss whether it was destined to failure from the start.
	
	2. Participate in a debate. Resolved: "German tradition prevented the acceptance of democracy in German society after World War I."
	
	3. View one or more of the following films. Discuss what each states about the condition of Weimar Germany and the reasons for its eventual downfall.
	
	  a. "The Cabinet of Dr. Caligari"
	  b. "M"
	  c. "Metropolis"
	  d. "The Blue Angel"
	  e. "Cabaret"
		One of the most fascinating ways to interpret the 1920's in Germany is to analyze the music, art, and especially films of the period. A basic analysis of these films will help recreate the mood of the 1930's in Germany and will focus on the persistent issues of mental illness, sadism, authority, anarchy, control, and murder in Weimar Germany.

	4. Read and discuss From Caligari to Hitler, by Siegfried Kracauer, pp. 63-65, 72-74, 162-194, 215-222. AA	Kracauer's psychoanalytic commentary is a compelling look at the nature and scope of the German film industry of the 1920's.
	5. Create a series of political cartoons which dramatize the problems encountered by the Weimar government. 6. Examine the drawings in "Weimar Art." (See THE ANTHOLOGY). - How do you react to what you have seen? - Compare Photomontages of the Nazi Period, by John Heartfield, a German Communist and gifted artist, to the other drawings.	These paintings and drawings show some of the dissatisfaction with the nature of the post-World War I era. While artists criticized war and the German past, they also believed that Weimar was not a change, but only more of the same in a different form.

PERFORMANCE OBJECTIVES	LEARNING ACTIVITIES/MATERIALS	COMMENTARY
4. The student will examine the broad appeal of Nazi philosophy and government.	1. Construct a list that shows the basic ideas and tenets of Nazism. Explain what they mean to you. 2. Read The Anatomy of Nazism, by Earl Raab and outline the major ideas of Nazi philosophers. AA 3. View the filmstrip, "The Anatomy of Nazism," and compare it to the readings you have completed. 4. Read "Hitler and the Nazis," in Nazi Germany, a Xerox (AEP Publication, pp. 22-25. Summarize your findings. A 5. Construct a dramatization in which a Nazi official and a member of the Jewish community discuss their views. 6. Read The True Believer, by Eric Hoffer, and prepare a wall mural, poster, or bulletin board display which illustrates how Hoffer's personality types were found in the Nazi movement. AA 7. Define the term, "value." Make a list of at least five "values" you hold. How is a value different from a mood, a whim, or a sensation? Examine your five values against the following checklist questions: - Did you choose this value freely from alternatives? - Did you consider the consequences? - Do you feel proud of the value? - Do you talk about it publicly? - Do you act consistently on this value? - How do you resolve conflicts among your values?	Deals with the motivation for participating in a mass movement. Some would argue that it is overly simplistic, ignores economic and social forces, and is status-quo oriented; however, the book is worth examining. Erich Kahler has defined a value as "a fundamental significance which we attach to matters of life, and through which we orient ourselves in our conduct." Values have permanence, are claimed valid for a human community, are derived from choice, and are acted upon consistently. It is crucial to identify the similarities and differences in people's values during an investigation of Nazism.

PERFORMANCE OBJECTIVES	LEARNING ACTIVITIES/MATERIALS	COMMENTARY
	8. Read and explain "What the Nazis Believed" (See ANTHOLOGY) A	
	9. Read "Tomorrow Belongs to Me," in How Democracy Failed, by Ellen Switzer (See ANTHOLOGY) - Why were the lyrics in this piece appealing to youth?	Important because it focuses upon the relationship between the rise of Nazism and young people.
	10. Examine the campaign poster (See ANTHOLOGY). - Even if you do not know German, what makes this design appealing?	
	11. Prepare a recruiting campaign which would provide the Nazi Party with a broader base of membership. Your campaign should include slogans, posters, art, music, speeches, which display a nationalistic fervor.	
	12. Read from among the following selections and explain how each selection you choose illustrates the broad appeal of Nazi philosophy and government.	
	a. "Halberg Goes Nazi," Xerox (AEP), Nazi Germany, pp. 27-45 A	A dramatic account of what happened in a typical German community to make average people accept Nazism.
	b. "Are the Germans Human?" in The Tragedy of Nazi Germany, by Peter Phillips, pp. 20-27. AA	An assessment of the "German character" as a possible explanation for the events of the period.
	c. Hitler: Great Lives Observed, by George Stein, pp. 94-105 A	An illuminating look at the almost religious devotion of people who followed Hitler.

PERFORMANCE OBJECTIVES	LEARNING ACTIVITIES/MATERIALS	COMMENTARY
	d. "Destiny's Tot" in The Fifty Minute Hour, by Robert Lindner, pp. 119-155. A	Fascinating account of a prison psychologist's attempt to understand the reasons behind a Nazi leader's rationale for joining the Nazi Party.
		The movie, Pressure Point, with Sidney Poitier as Dr. Lindner, and Bobby Darin as Anton, is worthwhile.
	e. "Short Talk With A Fascist Beast," in Man Alone, edited by Erie and Marx Josephson, pp. 388-393. A	An excellent reading for uncovering the sociological and economic motivations behind Nazism.
	f. "The Authoritarian Ideology of the Family in The Mass Psychology of Fascism," in The Mass Psychology of Fascism, by Wilhelm Reich. pp. 34-74. AA	Thesis: the linking of fascism and sexual frustrations.
	g. "The Racial Question," in Hitler's War Against the Jews, by David Altshuler, pp. 16-18 (See ANTHOLOGY) BA	Focuses upon how the Nazis used disease and contamination.
	h. "The Jews in Hitler's Mental World," pp. 3-22, and "Anti-Semitism in Modern Germany," pp. 23-47, in The War Against the Jews, by Lucy Dawidowicz. AA	Largely historic account of growth of anti-Semitism in Germany. Excellent detail; one of the basic texts on the Holocaust.
	i. "The Myth of the Jewish World Conspiracy," in Commentary, June, 1966, by Norman Cohn. AA	Offers a psychoanalytic theory of anti-Semitism.
	j. "German Racism, Hitler and the Protocols, pp. 169-193, and "The Myth in Nazi Propaganda," pp. 194-215, in Warrant For Genocide, by Norman Cohn. A	An excellent historical monograph of the origins and use of The Protocols of the Elders of Zion.

PERFORMANCE OBJECTIVES	LEARNING ACTIVITIES/MATERIALS	COMMENTARY
	k. The Painted Bird, by Jerzy Kosinski. A	A brutal account of a young boy's experiences in Eastern Europe and his attempt to survive prejudice and super-stition.
		This is an explosive, highly readable, and interesting novel. There are graphically violent scenes which might render this work objection-able to some people.
	l. The Last of the Just, by Andre Schwarz-Bart, pp. 148-155, 247-264. AA	These selections illustrate the irrational and savage behavior directed at Jews.
	m. Christians and Jews, by Rudolph M. Lowenstein, pp. 14-52. AA	Deals with the psychology of anti-Semitism.
	n. Read A Boy of Old Prague, by S. Ish-Kishor. BA	This is a description of a pogrom and a vivid example of personal prejudice.
	13. Examine the poster on "The Protocols of the Elders of Zion." Research the origins and use of "The Protocols" and then respond to the following questions. - When were the cartoons/posters published? - What do the posters claim? - What do the posters tell you about the climate of the time? - Explain the significance of the symbols used to describe the Jews. - Who uses them today? Why?	

PERFORMANCE OBJECTIVES	LEARNING ACTIVITIES/MATERIALS	COMMENTARY

14. View the following films and discuss their implications in relation to the issues of prejudice and inhumanity.

  a. "Puppets"

A stylized puppet actor provides a unique lesson on propaganda, conformity and totalitarianism. A good discussion of the use of scapegoat techniques to gain adherents.

  b. "Day in the Life of Jonathan Mole."

15. Comment on the following quotation from Simon Wiesenthal's The Sunflower: "A wise man once said that the Jews were the salt of the earth. But the Poles thought that their land had been ruined by over-salting."

16. In a role-play situation, demonstrate the "Big Lie" tactics and propaganda devices employed by the Nazis. After the demonstration, compare this style with contemporary advertising.

17. Read Twelve Year Reich: The Social History of Nazi Germany, 1933-1945, by Richard Grunberger. Discuss the diverse appeal of Nazi philosophy.   AA

A readable selection which shows the use of ritual and speech in providing symbolic support for a regime.

18. Read "Eichmannism," in Crazy Talk, Stupid Talk, by Neil Postman, pp. 178-186.   A

Another selection on the use of ritual and speech.

19. Invite a rabbi, priest, minister, or historian to discuss the origins of anti-Semitism in Germany. Consider why this appealed to certain segments of German society.

For a list of possible speakers, contact:

Anti-Defamation League of B'nai B'rith

20. Read the following statement from Who Should Play God? by
    Ted Howard and Jeremy Rifkin, p. 47   A

    Some day we will realize that the prime duty, the ines-
    capable duty of the good citizens of the right type is
    to leave his or her blood behind him in the world; and
    that we have no business to permit the perpetuation of
    citizens of the wrong type. The great problem of civiliza-
    tion is to secure a relative increase of the valuable as
    compared with the less valuable or noxious elements in
    the population...The problem cannot be met unless we give
    full consideration to the immense influence of heredity....
    I wish very much that the wrong people could be prevented
    entirely from breeding; and when the evil nature of these
    people is sufficiently flagrant, this should be done.
    Criminals should be sterilized and feebleminded persons
    forbidden to leave off-spring behind them...The emphasis
    should be laid on getting desirable people to breed.

    - What does this selection say?

    - Who do you think made this statement?

    - Do you agree with it?

21. Participate in a role-play in which you are a member of Joseph
    Goebbel's staff. Suggest new ways and techniques to instill
    Nazi loyalty, nationalism, and devotion to Hitler.

COMMENTARY

The Memorial Committee for
 the Six Million Jewish
 Martyrs,
Philadelphia, Pa.

After discussion, point out
that the author was
Theodore Roosevelt.
An American history class may
wish to explore what the
statement says about the
"progressive era" in the United
States.

PERFORMANCE OBJECTIVES	LEARNING ACTIVITIES/MATERIALS	COMMENTARY

	22. Read one of the following:
	
	   a. The Mind of Adolf Hitler, by Walter Langer, pp. 37–44
	           AA
		This is the classic wartime psychological study of Hitler's youth and motivating behavior. Use with Robert Waite's The Psychopathic God.

	b. "Heinrich Himmler, A Clinical Case of Anal-Hoarding Sadism," in The Anatomy of Human Destructiveness, by Erich Fromm. AA	A well written psychological interpretation with Fromm's "sobering conclusions that thousands of Himmlers exist in our society."
	c. "Lord and Master of His Troubled Era," in Hitler: Great Lives Observed, by Ernest Nolte, pp. 145–151. AA d. "The Psychopathic God," by Robert Waite, pp. 24–28 A After completion of the reading, write a report in which you are a psychiatrist profiling Hitler's character and personality. What aspects of his personality helped him to become the guiding force of the Nazi Party?	

	23. Read "The Rise of Fascism." (See ANTHOLOGY) A
	   – How do you react to the last two lines of Yeats's quotation?
	   – What was the basis for the rise of fascism?
		This reading points out that fascism was a worldwide movement, and that the values popular in Germany were also present in other nations.

	24. Read "The Message of the Nazis: Slogans, Posters, Songs and Games." (See ANTHOLOGY) A/BA – What are the most important values expressed in the slogans, symbols, and songs of the Nazis?	

PERFORMANCE OBJECTIVES	LEARNING ACTIVITIES/MATERIALS	COMMENTARY
5. The student will state and support generalizations about the reasons for the rise of the Nazi state.	1. In a small group, rank in descending order of importance, the major reasons for the rise of Nazism. Justify your ranking for the entire class. 2. Using Adolf Hitler and one additional dictator, thoroughly research their rise to power. Then, in an essay, provide an analysis of the reasons for their rise. Consider Stalin, Batista, Castro, Mao, Franco, Peron, Mussolini, Idi Amin, etc. 3. Participate in a debate on the following proposition: Resolved: "The Media Made the Third Reich." 4. Write a reaction to Eugene Anderson's sentiments that while German history failed to cultivate "democratic virtues," the rise of a German Nazi state was not inevitable. 5. Write a position paper which reflects your conclusions about the reasons for the rise of Nazism. 6. Construct a bulletin board, collage, or poster display in which you illustrate the reasons for Hitler's rise to power. 7. Given conditions similar to those in Germany in 1932, participate in a small group simulation in which you create a master plan for the takeover of the government. Incorporate into your master plan the use of the media, law and institutions, and psychological appeals to the masses to attain and maintain power. - How does your simulated master plan relate to the actual plan developed by the Nazis? In a large group, compare and contrast the plans developed with those of Adolf Hitler. 8. Adolf Hitler, at one time, made the following statement: "A woman must be a cute,naive, little thing –tender, sweet and stupid." - How does this statement fit into basic Nazi thought?	

PERFORMANCE OBJECTIVES	LEARNING ACTIVITIES/MATERIALS	COMMENTARY
	9. Examine the following oath taken by a German child entering the Hitler Youth at age 14: "In the presence of the Blood flag which represents our Fuhrer, I swear to devote all my energies, all my strength to the savior of our country, Adolf Hitler. I am willing and ready to give up my life for him, so help me God. One Volk, one Reich, one Fuhrer." Analyze this oath and compare it with others. What is the significance of an oath? Why would the Nazis encourage the taking of oaths by children and adults?	
	10. Who made the following statement? "The streets of our country are in turmoil. The universities are filled with students rebelling and rioting. Communists are seeking to destroy our country. Russia is threatening her with her might. And the republic is in danger. Yes, danger from within and without. We need law and order. Yes, without law and order our nation cannot survive.... We shall restore law and order."	This statement is attributed to Adolf Hitler in 1932 or 1933.
	11. Read the account of Leo Frank rape case in Tom Watson: Agrarian Rebel, by C. Vann Woodward, pp. 435-449. A - Why did such cases incur intense wrath from the whites? - Compare what happened to Leo Frank with what happened in Germany.	Leo Frank, a Jew, was accused of the murder of 14-year-old Mary Phagan in Atlanta, Georgia, on April 27, 1913. He was ultimately lynched although never proven guilty of the crime.
	12. View the film, "Hitler." - To what extent was Hitler personally responsible for the rise of the Nazi state?	The student should re-evaluate any conclusions in this area at the end of the course.

PERFORMANCE OBJECTIVES	LEARNING ACTIVITIES/MATERIALS	COMMENTARY
	13. Comment on the following statement by Rollo May: "Deeds of violence in our society are performed largely by those trying to establish their self-esteem, to defend their self-image, and to demonstrate that they, too, are significant...violence arises not out of superfluity of power but out of powerlessness." - How might this apply to the rise of Nazism?	
	14. Respond to "Why Did the Nazis Come to Power in Germany" (See ANTHOLOGY) A - Write your response in essay form.	
	15. Read "The Rise of Hitler." (See ANTHOLOGY) Fully discuss the economic implications of Nazism.	
	16. Respond to each of the dilemmas in "Decision-Making: Pre-Nazi Germany" (See ANTHOLOGY)	Each of the dilemmas in this selection requires a difficult choice. After students have responded to all of them, they might draw conclusions about how they feel most Germans would have responded.
	17. Read "Jewish Life in Twentieth Century Europe." (See ANTHOLOGY) AA - Explain how the Jewish people contributed to both Polish and German culture. - How did some Germans perceive the effect of the Jews on the economic and cultural life of Germany?	This brief selection should make clear to students that Jews were not only historical victims, but were a thriving people who not only possessed their own culture, but were making contributions to Western civilization.

UNIT IV: FROM PERSECUTION TO MASS MURDER

INTRODUCTION

In this unit the student will examine the German decision to murder millions of people in what was called the "Final Solution." Each step of this process is treated, including the Einsatzgruppen on the Eastern front, the early experiments with euthanasia and diesel gas, ghettoization, and the gas chambers of the death camps. Life in the death camps and in the ghettos is analyzed, especially as it related to the psychological consequences of surviving under such stressful conditions. The student will investigate how efficiency and terror merged to produce the largest technology of death in the twentieth century, an investigation in which he/she will clarify how industry cooperated with and benefited from the system. The fact that the "Final Solution" was not the work of insane people, but the cold, bureaucratic result of a large number of respectable, middle-class people carrying out a businesslike order, should be clear.

<u>UNIT GOAL</u>: The implementation of the Nazi philosophy
resulted in the rise of a totalitarian state, a policy of
mass murder, phenomenal stress, and diverse responses as people
struggled to survive.

<u>PERFORMANCE OBJECTIVES</u>:

1. The student will examine Nazi policies in the years
    immediately following their rise to power.

2. The student will describe life in Nazi Germany.

3. The student will examine the escalation of Nazi perse-
    cution policies, and responses to them, which included
    conformity and defiance.

4. The student will reassess her/his generalizations about
    human nature in light of The events in Nazi Germany.

Arbeit Macht Frei	The deceptive slogan over the gates of Auschwitz which meant "Work Makes Free." The slogan, originally in French, was created by the founder of the International Labor Organization and had a positive connotation.
Auschwitz	A town in southwestern Poland which was the site of the infamous Nazi concentration and death camp in World War II.
Babi Yar	The ravine in the Ukraine where 90,000 Jews were marched into pits and machine gunned to death.
Buber, Martin	The Jewish philosopher who conceived of religious faith as being a dialogue between man and God; has deeply influenced modern Christian theology.
Buna-Werke	A factory which produced synthetic rubber at Auschwitz.
Canada	The unit responsible for clothing and all supplies at Auschwitz.
crematoria	The furnaces used to burn dead bodies in the death camps.
Einsatzgruppen	The special military SS units used in Eastern Europe to round up and kill large number of Jews.
Final Solution	The plan instituted by the Reich to provide for the systematic mass murder of every Jew in Europe.
Grynszpan, Herschel	The half-crazed assassin of the Nazi diplomat, Third Secretary Ernst Vom Rath.
Heydrich, Reinhard	The Nazi leader known as the "Blonde Beast" who headed the Gestapo until his assassination. Lidice, Czecho-slovakia, was destroyed to avenge his death.
Hoess, Rudolph	The Commandant at Auschwitz, who was convicted of war crimes at Nuremberg and executed.
I. G. Farben	The German chemical and pharmaceutical conglomerate which used death camp slave labor.
Judenrein	The German term meaning to make "clean of Jews."
Kiddush Hashem	Hebrew for the sanctification of God's name; martyrdom rather than renunciation of one's beliefs.
Kristallnacht	A planned, "spontaneous," nationwide retaliation, Nov. 9-10, 1938, against the Jews for the assassination of Ernst Vom Rath. The streets were covered with broken glass; hence, the name, "Crystal Night."

Madagascar Plan	The short-lived German plan to send all Jews to the African island of Madagascar for permanent residence, which was replaced by the Final Solution.
Mengele, Dr. Joseph	The man responsible for selecting those who were to die at Auschwitz, and was responsible for "medical experiments" on inmates. He is the subject of Ira Levin's book, The Boys From Brazil, and is still alive and at large.
Mischlinge	The "mixed" offspring of German Christians and Jews. Special laws applied to them. Most survived.
Mussulmanner	The concentration camp inmates who were so sick and emaciated that they literally became the "walking dead."
Nuremberg Laws	The series of laws instituted by the Third Reich to drastically and systematically restrict the political, social and economic life of German Jews.
psychic numbing	A term used by Bruno Bettelheim to describe a defense mechanism by which emotion is desensitized to allow people to survive overwhelmingly painful situations.
regression	The psychological return to an earlier stage of behavior.
"resettlement"	The Nazi debasement of language meaning "sent to a concentration camp."
Shtetl	The Yiddish term for village.
Sonderkommando	The detachments of male Jews assigned responsibility for the mechanics of execution and body disposal within the death camps.
"special treatment"	The coded language meaning the process of annihilation of the Jewish and non-Aryan population by the Nazis.
sterilization	The act or process of rendering an individual incapable of producing children which was used by the Nazis as part of the eugenics program against "lower" peoples.
Treblinka	A death camp in Poland, northeast of Warsaw, which was destroyed by inmates in the Treblinka Revolt.
Ubermensch.	The "German Superman," an idea which originally entered Nazi thinking through a corruption of Nietzsche's philosophy.
Umschlagplatz	The railroad loading platform from which Jews were sent to concentration camps.

Untermenschen   Those individuals who were considered to be genetically
                         inferior to the "Aryan race" by the Nazis.

Vom Rath, Ernst   The Reich's Third Secretary in Paris shot by a 17-year
                         old German Jew, Herschel Grynspan.

"Wear the Yellow   The famous Zionist editorial of 1933 which called on
 Badge With Pride"   Jews to reject assimilation and self-hate, and to dis-
                         play their Jewishness with pride.

Yellow Star   The identifying symbol which Jews were required to
                         wear on their clothing; yellow was considered the
                         color of shame.

Youth Aliyah   A Zionist group which encouraged young Jews to move
                         to Palestine.

Zyklon B   The insecticide used by the Nazis to kill the Jews
                         more efficiently in the death camps.

UNIT IV: <u>UNIT GOAL</u>:   The implementation of the Nazi philosophy resulted in the rise of a totalitarian
          state, a policy of   mass murder, phenomenal stress, and diverse responses as people struggled to survive.

PERFORMANCE OBJECTIVES	LEARNING ACTIVITIES/MATERIALS	COMMENTARY
1. The student will examine Nazi policies in the years immediately following their rise to power.	1. Read at least one of the following: a. "Anti-Jewish Legislation 1933-1938" and "Between Freedom and Ghetto: The Jews in Germany, 1933-1938," in <u>War Against the Jews</u>, by Lucy Dawidowicz, pp. 48-69, 164-196. AA b. <u>The Holocaust</u> and <u>The Holocaust and Resistance</u>, Yad Vashem pamphlets. A c. "Manipulating the Law," in <u>Hitler's War Against the Jews</u>, by David Altshuler, pp. 44-46. (See ANTHOLOGY) BA - Using the readings you have completed, compile a list of specific Nazi policies; explain those policies. 2. View one or more of the following films or filmstrips. Note the rise of Hitler in 1933. a. "From Kaiser to Fuhrer" b. "The Twisted Cross" c. "Mein Kampf" d. "Rise and Fall of Adolf Hitler" (four-part filmstrip) - Using the media you select, explain the rise of Hitler. 3. The year is 1935. You are a candidate for the office of President of the United States. Prepare a position paper on "Human Rights in Nazi Germany." 4. Prepare a time-line of major laws aimed at German Jews from 1933-1935.	Please note that ANTHOLOGY refers to THE HOLOCAUST AND GENOCIDE: A SEARCH FOR CON-SCIENCE; AN ANTHOLOGY FOR STUDENTS. Detailed accounts of the early Nazi years, and the response of the Jews in Germany. Explains early Aryan legisla-tion. Clearly describes the early anti-Jewish legislation by the Nazis, including the Nuremberg Laws.

PERFORMANCE OBJECTIVES	LEARNING ACTIVITIES/MATERIALS	COMMENTARY
	5. Write a newspaper article on the Nuremberg Laws; include the laws passed, personal reactions from German citizens, reactions from German Jews, and the American reaction to these laws. Be sure to maintain historical accuracy in your account.	
	6. Role-play a series of interviews with several German citizens in which you solicit their reaction to the Nuremberg Laws: a. A shopkeeper b. A German Socialist c. An S. A. member d. An ex-army officer e. A teacher in the university f. A German Jew	
2. The student will describe life in Nazi Germany	1. Read one or more of the following. Write a letter of a diary account in which you describe a typical day or days in Nazi Germany.	
	a. "Life Under Nazism," in <u>Anatomy of Nazism</u>, by Earl Raab, pp. 11-12. A	Summary of the quality of life in the early Nazi era.
	b. <u>Nazi Culture</u>, by George Mosse, pp. 39-47, 341-345, 271-276, 281-282, 284-293. A	Selections which include Nazi views on women and what it meant to be part of a movement.
	c. <u>The Twelve Year Reich</u>, by Richard Grunberger, pp. 79-98, 240-292, 356-363, 431-501. A	Excellent sections on Fuhrer worship, the family, Nazi speech and culture.
	d. <u>Inside the Third Reich</u>, by Albert Speer, pp. 41-62, 64-85. AA	The noted Nazi explains his early career and success-orientation as reasons for joining the Nazi Party.

PERFORMANCE OBJECTIVES	LEARNING ACTIVITIES/MATERIALS	COMMENTARY
	e. I Was There, by Hans Richter. BA	An account of what it was like in Germany, from the point of view of a member of Hitler Youth.
	2. Present an oral report on the origins, beliefs, practices and leadership of the SS. Refer to SS and Gestapo, by Roger Manvell, and The Order of the Death's Head, by Heinz Hohne. AA	
	3. Read the poem, "SS Man," by Bob Rosenbloom A - Discuss your feelings after reading this short piece.	
	4. As a public relations person for the SS, prepare a pamphlet in which you explain the philosophy of the SS and its critical functions.	
	5. Read Of Pure Blood, by Marc Hillel (Chapter 3, "Bearing Children for the Fuhrer"). Write a report in which you describe the importance of this program to the Nazi regime.	
	6. Conduct a series of role-play interviews with German citizens in which you obtain their views about the quality of life in the "New Germany": a. An old Prussian soldier b. An executive of an armaments factory c. A factory worker d. A Protestant minister e. A small child.	
	7. Participate in the simulation "Gestapo." - One of the student activities which has been utilized in conjunction with the Holocaust unit is a simulation experience called "Gestapo." Prior to full class participation in that exercise, several students are "secretly recruited" by the teacher to role play "Gestapo agents." The rest of the class is not informed about the identity of the agents; the agents are briefed on the game to be played over the next three or four days.	

After the agents are established and briefed, the teacher intro-
duces the simulation game. The students are told that they are
not permitted to use the pronoun "I" at any time during class
(and are advised not to use it outside of class either, since
they do not know who or where the agents are). They are told
that Gestapo agents have been secretly appointed, and that those
agents will report the names of any students who commit infractions of the simple rule set down. The students are also
reminded to be careful of what they say at all times, since
they can never be certain of who is or is not an agent. The
list of offenders will be presented secretly to the teacher
prior to each subsequent class period - and the teacher will
publicly list those names on the chalkboard along with the
number of times the student has committed the offense. The game
begins that class period with the agents secretly recording
the infractions as the normal class activities proceed. (Agents
are given complete freedom to report on classmates in class
or outside of class, and to recruit other persons-- not
students in the class itself--to help them catch offenders.
No rules about accuracy or honesty are set down for the agents;
they are assured of complete support-- without question-- by
the teacher.)

When the class reports for the next day, the teacher lists the
offenders, and establishes punishment for those who have committed infractions above an "acceptable" limit (perhaps 5 or 6
times). All offending students are required to fully participate in whatever regular class activities are taking place,
but they must STAND for the entire period.

On the third day, the same procedure is followed, but the punishment for offenders increases in intensity. Offending students
are required to write, "I will obey the agents and the system,"
a minimum of two-hundred times-- or for the full period --
during class. Other students go on with regular class
activities.

On the final day of simulated activity, offenders (and "repeaters") are listed on the board and all who have offended are told that they must give up ALL of their free time in school (lunch, study halls, etc.) for the next week (as well as 30 minutes before and 30 minutes after school) to participate in a school "cleanup" campaign. This part of the simulation works best if reinforced by the appearance of a building administrator who has the authority to actually hand down such disciplinary measures to the students.

<u>Reactions at this point may become excessive...and it is time to halt the play and debrief.</u>

The students must be told that the "cleanup" was simply part of the simulation, that the administrator was also only "playing a role" in the game, and that the simulation is now over. In the debriefing which is conducted, the students should be encouraged to explain how they feel at the moment - and how they felt during the playing of the game. Relationships can easily be drawn to the "mood" in Nazi Germany-- or at other times when oppression has been present within a given society.

-Students should realize the "paranoia" which built up in them, the power which the "agents" assumed-- usually far beyond that which was "permitted" -- the dangers of the abuse/misuse of power, the "terror" of always being watched, etc.

Conclude by reminding students that this was simply a simulation game among friends and peers. Have them try to imagine that Nazi Germany must have really been like....

8. Read "Totalization and Terror," in <u>The Tower and the Abyss</u>, by Erich Kahler, pp. 62-78.   AA
   - List and explain the terror tactics used by the Nazis.

9. Read _The Twelve Year Reich: The Social History of Nazi Germany, 1933-1945_, by Richard Grunberger, pp. 269-273 and 420-424.   A

   - Write a report in which you discuss the Nazi attitudes toward sexuality and homosexuality.

10. Assume the role of a German youth; explain to your parents why you want to join the Hitler Youth Organization.

11. With another student, construct two newspapers that illustrate life under the Nazis. Include editorials, advertisements, obituaries, cartoons, and other pertinent information. One should demonstrate a pro-Nazi viewpoint, and the other anti-Nazi sentiments.

12. A popular Jewish teacher in your school has just been replaced by a member of the Nazi Party. A Jewish parent has questioned the replacement.

   - Assume the role of the building principal and explain this action.

13. Prepare a bulletin board display or a wall mural in which you depict one of the following:

   a. Hitler Youth
   b. "Strength Through Joy"
   c. Science and Technological Achievement
   d. German Nationalism
   e. Anti-Jewish Propaganda
   f. Body Development and the 1936 Olympics

14. Play the role of a German sportswriter and write a column in which you explain the success of Jesse Owens in the 1936 Olympics.

15. Assume the role of a Nazi censor and prepare a radio broadcast in response to the following:

   a. The Declaration of Independence
   b. Ku Klux Klan literature
   c. _Hustler_ magazine
   d. Freudian psychology.

PERFORMANCE OBJECTIVES	LEARNING ACTIVITIES/MATERIALS	COMMENTARY
	16. Read selections from <u>The Third Reich of Dreams</u>, by Charlotte Beradt. A - Write an essay in which you discuss what dreams tell you about the state of the individual living in a totalitarian society.	
	17. View "The Hand." Discuss the meaning of the film in relation to the nature of totalitarianism.	A brilliant animated short story about a young man who loves flowers. One day, his life is interrupted and changed forever by "The Hand."
	18. Read "Albert Speer," in <u>Discover Magazine</u>, <u>Sunday Bulletin,</u> July 31, 1977. A	Hitler's Minister of Armaments talks candidly about The Third Reich.
	19. Read "The Jungvolk/The Way To School," (See ANTHOLOGY) BA - Describe the "mood" in the early years of Nazi Germany.	Explores the mood of the early years in Nazi Germany.
	20. Respond to "An Olympic Athlete's Dilemma." (See ANTHOLOGY)	The 1936 Olympic Games in Berlin were a major Nazi propaganda event. This dilemma should help the student draw parallels with the 1980 Moscow Olympics.

	21. Read "The Search for Countries of Refuge: The Evian Conference" (See ANTHOLOGY) A
	
	  - What agreements were reached at the Evian Conference? Why were they important?
	
	  - Did Americans have the right to judge what happened at Evian?
		In 1938, 32 nations met to discuss the "Jewish Question." The students should react to the results of the conference as described in this excellent selection from Arthur Morse's <u>While Six Million Died.</u>

22. Examine the survey results recorded in "American Views on
The Refugee Question." (See ANTHOLOGY) BA
- How do you account for these results?
- What conclusions can be drawn from them?

23. Read "The Munich Conference." (See ANTHOLOGY).   A

- Evaluate Chamberlain's attitude and actions at the Munich
Conference.

3. The student will
examine the escala-
tion of Nazi per-
secution policies,
and the responses
to them, which in-
clude conformity
and defiance.

1. Research newspaper and other accounts of Kristallnacht. Write
two press releases, one from the SS and the other from a
small Jewish printer, in which you react to the events which
took place.

2. Read and discuss, "The Jewish Response to Crisis," in Hitler's
War Against the Jews, by David Altshuler, pp. 170-179. BA

3. Read and react to one or more of the following selections
about German mass executions:

a. "Solomon Tauber in Riga," in The Odessa File, by Frederick
Forsyth, pp. 27-67. (See ANTHOLOGY) A

b. "Mass Executions," in The Yellow Star, by Gerhard Schoenberger, pp. 105-128. BA

c. "Death at Dubno, 1942 " (See ANTHOLOGY)   A

4. Read one or more of the following selections about life in the
ghetto of Eastern Europe. Write a short story in which you
comment upon that life.

a. "The Warsaw Ghetto," in The Holocaust, by Bea Stadtler.
(See ANTHOLOGY) BA

This selection contains one
very poignant moment when a
man helped his wife into the
gas van.

Dramatic photographs and
primary source materials.

b. "Death and Life in the Eastern European Ghetto," in The War Against the Jews, by Lucy Dawidowicz, pp. 197-222. A

Excellent account of the later years of Nazi extermination policy.

c. 'In the Ghettos" and "The Deportations," in The Yellow Star, by Gerhard Schoenberger, pp. 67-102, pp. 129-168.   A

d. "The Judenrat Government," in The Holocaust, by Bea Stadtler pp. 35-42. (SEE ANTHOLOGY)   BA

e. 'The Official Community: From Kehilla to Judenrat," in The War Against the Jews, by Lucy Dawidowicz, pp. 223-241. A

f. "Introduction," in Judenrat, by Isaiah Trunk.   AA

The major account of the function and activities of the Jewish Ghetto organization.

g. Never To Forget, by Milton Meltzer, pp. 49-135.   A

h. Read "Hunger Is My Father" translated by Murray J. Kohn in The Voice of My Blood Cries Out.   (See ANTHOLOGY)

5. Participate in the "Judenrat" simulation.

You are a member of the Judenrat in the Warsaw Ghetto. With the other members of that Council, you must select five of your own people in the ghetto to be removed for transport to an extermination camp.

The Judenrat has been called into session to discuss the people who are listed below as "possible candidates" for removal and eventual extermination. In your Council, decide upon the five people which you as the Judenrat will remove from the ghetto and send to the extermination camp tomorrow morning.

PERFORMANCE OBJECTIVES	LEARNING ACTIVITIES/MATERIALS	COMMENTARY
	1. RABBI — He is 55 years of age and the spiritual leader of the community.	
	2. ADAM — His daughter is married to a member of the Third Reich. Through his daughter, he is able to get extra food and supplies for those living in the ghetto.	
	3. JOSEPH — He is the physician for the ghetto; 48 years of age.	
	4. YEHUDITH — She is a 7-year-old orphan whose parents were killed during the uprising.	
	5. HANNAH — She is a 30-year-old prostitute who provides "services" to the Nazis in exchange for food and clothing for the people in the ghetto.	
	6. MORDECHAI — He is a violinist who speaks fluent German; he has been most successful in hearing about and knowing the Nazi plans for the ghetto before they are implemented. (Mordechai will not leave the ghetto without his wife, Sarah).	
	7. SARAH — She is the wife of Mordechai, and is six months pregnant. (She will not leave the ghetto without her husband.)	
	8. SAMUEL — He is a 28-year-old strong muscle man. He has been able to protect the other people in the ghetto by assuming the physical abuse which would be directed toward others.	
	9. HYAM — He is a 35-year-old scholar, artist, and literary expert. He is keeping all of the records, art, memoirs, and journals of experiences in the ghetto.	
	10. VICTOR — He is a 17-year-old activist who seems to hold the people in the ghetto together with his spirit, his hope, his youth, and his conviction.	

PERFORMANCE OBJECTIVES	LEARNING ACTIVITIES/MATERIALS	COMMENTARY
	6. Read "Concentration and Death Camps." Explain their location. Research and describe the difference between a concentration camp and a death camp (See ANTHOLOGY). BA/A	
	7. Read two or more of the following selections about life in the concentration camps. React to what you have read, in writing.	
	a. Night, by Elie Wiesel, pp. 39-81 (See ANTHOLOGY) A	The classic short autobiographical novel about Auschwitz; excellent for students who have little knowledge of the Holocaust.
	b. Man's Search for Meaning, by Viktor Frankl. (See ANTHOLOGY) A	The author's account of his own experiences in Auschwitz.
	c. "Behavior in Extreme Situations: Coercion," "Behavior in Extreme Situations: Defense," "The Fluctuating Price of Life," "Men Are Not Ants," in The Informed Heart, by Bruno Bettleheim, pp. 108-174, 175-341, 232-254, 260-292. AA	The author discusses the effects of the camp upon individual behavior.
	d. "The Excremental Assault," "Nightmare and Washing," and "Life In Death," in The Survivor, by Terrence Des Pres, pp. 51-72, 73-94, 95-144. A	This response to Bruno Bettleheim pieces together primary accounts of life in the camps.
	e. The Investigation, by Peter Weiss, pp. 8-28, 44-65, 55-63, 112-117, 184-193. A	
	f. "The Drowned and the Saved," in Survival in Auschwitz, by Primo Levi, pp. 79-91. AA	Compares the various means of survival in a number of death camps.
	g. Treblinka, by Jean-Francois Steiner, pp. 182-242, 311-411. A	An excellent docunovel on the famous death camp; especially the latter part which deals with the preparation for revolt.

PERFORMANCE OBJECTIVES	LEARNING ACTIVITIES/MATERIALS	COMMENTARY
	h. "The Extermination Camps," in The Yellow Star, by Gerhard Schoenberger, pp. 169-208. A	
	i. "Annihilation Camps," in The War Against the Jews, by Lucy Dawidowicz, pp. 129-149. A	
	j. Auschwitz, by Miklos Nyszli, pp. 29-31, 42-40, 120-135. AA	
	8. Research the number of Jews killed in Germany compared with other parts of Europe. - What conclusions can you draw from these comparisons?	
	9. View the film, "The Shop on Main Street." In a large group, discuss how the older woman's situation can be of great benefit to her helper.	This brilliant film reduces the terror of the Nazi era to the personal situation of an old Jewish woman, played by Ida Kamenska, and her Protestant helper, who can gain from her absence.
	10. Using poetry, music, or art, prepare an oral presentation focusing on the methods used by artists to portray the emotions of the concentration camps and ghetto inmates.	
	11. View one of more of the following films and discuss the film maker's view(s) of Nazi persecution.	
	a. "Night and Fog"	Alan Resnais' classic of the gradual process to the Final Solution. Stark.
	b. "Warsaw Ghetto"	An account of life in the most famous of ghettos.
	c. "Memorandum"	
	d. "Genocide"	Historically describes the murder process.

PERFORMANCE OBJECTIVES	LEARNING ACTIVITIES/MATERIALS	COMMENTARY
	e. "The Jewish Wife"	Brecht's play on film; with Viveca Lindfors.
	f. "Seven Beauties"	Lena Wertmuller's controversial film which, in part, shows her interpretation of life in the death camps. See the review in _Human Behavior_, May, 1976, or Bruno Bettleheim's brilliant critique in the book, _Surviving_. "Seven Beauties" was attacked as a film which distorted camp experience and choices.
	12. Listen to and/or interview one or more Holocaust victims. Prepare an oral history project of the experience.	The student should be formally trained in interview techniques prior to participation in the oral history project.
	13. View works of art and artifacts from the Holocaust. Write an essay in which you describe their meaning in terms of understanding the Holocaust.	
	14. Construct a bulletin board in which you illustrate life in the camps.	
	15. Write a letter as an SS guard in which you explain your job and daily life at a camp.	
	16. Role-play an interview with a Kapo. Discuss his duties and his reasons for performing them.	
	17. Role-play a camp inmate. Write a diary entry in which you express your feelings about the possibility of death.	
	18. Participate in a panel discussion in which you and classmates role-play survivors of the Holocaust. Fully examine your motivations and methods for survival.	

PERFORMANCE OBJECTIVES	LEARNING ACTIVITIES/MATERIALS	COMMENTARY
	19. Read and analyze the poem, "Babi Yar," by Yevgeny Yevtush-henko, in _The Holocaust Years: Society On Trial_, by Roselle Chartock and Jack Spencer. A	
	20. Discuss the following quotation by David Rousset: "Normal men do not know that everything is possible. Even if the evidence forces their intelligence to admit it, their muscles do not believe it. The concentrationees **do** know...they are set apart from the rest of the world by an experience impossible to communicate."	
	21. Read the selection dealing the the Jewish concept of "Kiddush Hashem," in _Hitler's War Against the Jews,_ by David Altshuler BA - How does the concept relate to decisions made during the Holocaust?	Students may be asked to compare "Kiddush Hashem" with the response of Christian slaves in the gladiator ring.
	22. Research the role of scientists and engineers in the Third Reich. Following the research, write an essay of formal report in which you assess their responsibility for the abuses committed during the Holocaust.	
	23. Examine the twenty exhibit posters of "The Holocaust, 1933-1945" published by the Anti-Defamation League. - Describe your emotional reactions.	
	24. Obtain a copy of "Journal of Testimony," an oral history of survivors of the Holocaust done in the Cleveland Heights, Ohio school system. A - Read excerpts and record your reactions.	
	25. Jessica Mitford, in _Kind and Usual Punishment_, argued that convicts have been used by major drug companies as "experi-mental material" for their drugs. Prisoners are paid approxi-mately one dollar a day for their participation. Unfortunately, there is much permanent damage to the "volunteers."	

PERFORMANCE OBJECTIVES	LEARNING ACTIVITIES/MATERIALS	COMMENTARY
	A group of black prisoners suffering from syphilis were divided into two groups; one group was given a placebo which condemned them to the mutilating effects of the disease. Doctors used them to study the process of deterioration. - How do you feel about these experiments?	
	26. Georgia welfare authorities sterilized several mentally deficient black girls. Their illiterate parents were allegedly compelled by the welfare bureaucracy to sign papers permitting the sterilization. - How do you react to this? - Should involuntary sterilization ever be permitted? Explain.	
	27. Discuss how the meaning of the following terms were manipulated. by the Nazis: resettlement special treatment concentration camp Final Solution selection	Students should understand how easily language can be used to distort reality; they might relate this to some circumstances in their own culture.
	28. Read. "The Holocaust," in <u>Discover Magazine</u>, <u>Sunday Bulletin,</u> July 17, 1977. A - Summarize what you have read.	
	29. Respond to the dilemma, "Race Defilement," (See ANTHOLOGY)	Those with mixed marriages faced special problems in Germany; the student should react to Gottshalk's eventual decision.
	30. Read "Honor the Yellow Badge," "Canonical and Nazi anti-Jewish Measures, and Pre-Nazi and Nazi anti-Jewish measures." (See ANTHOLOGY) A	These could motivate a discussion of how Jews might have responded to Nazi oppression in the early years. The second selection focuses on the continuity between earlier church edicts and Nazi actions.

PERFORMANCE OBJECTIVES	LEARNING ACTIVITIES/MATERIALS	COMMENTARY
	31. Respond to "David Rosenstein's Dilemma" (See ANTHOLOGY)	
	32. Read "The Night of Broken Glass" (See ANTHOLOGY). A	Kristallnacht was a major turning point in Nazi policies toward Jews.
	- How do you explain the violent and destructive nature of Kristallnacht? - How do you react to responses by police and civilians?	
	33. Read "Early Attacks in Poland: - Eric Dorf's Diary; -Everything Else Must Be Left Behind." (See ANTHOLOGY) A	As the war began with the attack on Poland, Jews were immediately subject to physical attack.
	-Write a "letter to the editor" in which you react to these readings.	
	34. Read "Euthanasia Program" (See ANTHOLOGY) BA	This selection provides a good account of the first experiments by the Nazis in using gas to kill people.
	- Explain how much you feel the German people knew about this program.	
	35. Respond to "The Shopkeeper's Dilemma" (See ANTHOLOGY) A	An examination of the excruciating position in which the Judenrats were placed.
	36. Read "The SS" (See ANTHOLOGY) A and Read "Nazi Leadership" (See ANTHOLOGY) BA	The SS was an elite group for which many Germans volunteered; many of those in the Nazi hierarchy were educated people.
	- What is particularly revealing about the chart of Nazi leaders?	
	37. Examine the chart of "Nazi Language" (See ANTHOLOGY) BA	Words can deceive, and the Nazis masked much of the reality of their actions behind deceptive language.
	- What is the danger in this kind of language usage?	

PERFORMANCE OBJECTIVES	LEARNING ACTIVITIES/MATERIALS	COMMENTARY

	38. Read "Punishment in the Camps." (See ANTHOLOGY) A
	
	   - How do you feel when you read about this kind of humiliation?
	
	   - How do you perceive the responses of the people?
		These excellent selections from Jean-Francois Steiner's <u>Treblinka</u> and Isabella Leitner's <u>Fragments of Isabella</u> show how individuals were punished in the camps.

	39. Read "The Death Process." (See ANTHOLOGY) A - What was the "Reality" of death process knowledge outside the camps?	This offers eyewitness testimony to the "Death Process" in the camps.

	40. Read "The Man With the Pink Triangle." (See ANTHOLOGY) A
	   - Why were special rules applied to homosexuals in the camps?
	   - How do you react to the persecution of homosexuals?
	
	41. Read "The Plight of the Gypsies." (See ANTHOLOGY) A/AA
	   - Why were Gypsies selected for persecution?
	
	   - Compare and contrast their treatment with that of other groups.
		The subject of homosexuals in the Holocaust has been virtually ignored. This selection from a recent work by Heinz Hagar offers some testimony about the treatment of homosexuals in the concentration camps.

	42. Read "Jehovah's Witnesses." (See ANTHOLOGY) A
	
	   - How do you respond to the actions of the Witnesses in the camps?
	   - Why are the Witnesses there in the first place?
		This selection about those who wore the purple triangle in the camps is taken from the autobiography of Commander Hoess of Auschwitz.

	43. Read "Nazi Medical Experiments." (See ANTHOLOGY) A
	
	   - How did the Nazi doctors justify their experiments both during and after the war?
	
	   - How do you react to the justification?
		A graphic and disturbing eyewitness account of what went on in many camps. Teachers are cautioned to use this with discretion due to the explicit and potentially offensive descriptions. The second part of the reading contains a discussion of research into the motivations of Nazi doctors.

44. Examine the drawings in "Art of the Camp Inmates"
    (See ANTHOLOGY)
    - What do these drawings reveal about the thoughts and
      feelings of the artists?

45. Read "I.G. Farben" (See ANTHOLOGY) A
    - Do corporations have an ethical responsibility which
      is "higher" than earning a profit? Explain.

Consider the role of big
business in the operation
of the concentration camps.

46. Read "Religious Faith in the Holocaust" (See ANTHOLOGY) A

    - How do you explain the role of God in the lives of camp
      inmates?

The selection, taken from
Elie Wiesel's Night, should
motivate a discussion about
the role of God in the lives
of those in the camps.

47. Read "Buchenwald and Dachau," in The Washington Post,
    April 10, 1977.   A
    - Summarize what you have read.
    - Why are eyewitness accounts important?

This article provides ex-
tensive commentary by
death camp survivors.

48. Imagine you are a Red Cross volunteer visiting one of the
    concentration camps during the war. Describe what you might
    have written in your report.

Students should understand
that the only camp visited
by the Red Cross was Therie-
sanstadt, which was "toned
down" for propaganda purposes.
Thus, the idea of an "in-
spection visit" to Treblinka
or Auschwitz would be
fantasy.

49. Invite several theologians to your class to explain the Judeo-
    Christian concepts of God.

    - Discuss the concepts of God in relation to the Holocaust.

Activities which relate to the
Supreme Being are by defini-
tion controversial. However,
such an issue cannot be ignored in a study of the
Holocaust.

PERFORMANCE OBJECTIVES	LEARNING ACTIVITIES/MATERIALS	COMMENTARY

	50. Read one or more of the following; react to what you have read, in writing.
	
	    a. _Night_, by Elie Wiesel. A
	
	    b. "Job: Our Contemporary," in _Messengers of God_, by Elie Wiesel, pp. 226-249. AA
	
	    c. "Lost and Found Again," by Elie Wiesel, in _Commonweal_ July, 1974, pp. 384-386. AA
	
	    d. "Looking Evil in the Eye," in _Time_, December 18, 1978, pp. 51-52. AA
		Wiesel interprets the story of the Biblical character who at first stood up to God's vengeful actions.
		
		Wiesel's explanation of where God was while the Jews suffered in the death camps. The issue of God is central to Wiesel.

	51. Play John Lennon's "God" and the classic Holocaust chant "Ani Maamin" Compare these two pieces for their viewpoints about the existence of God.	
	52. Debate: "Resolved: The existence of a Supreme Being and an event like the Holocaust are totally incompatible."	
	53. Write the script for a dramatization in which a concentration camp inmate prepares a series of questions for God. In your script, include the responses from God. You may share your views in a class discussion or act out your dramatization.	

PERFORMANCE OBJECTIVES	LEARNING ACTIVITIES/MATERIALS	COMMENTARY
	54. Comment on the following quotation from Andre Schwarz-Bart's, <u>The Last of the Just</u>: "Oh God, cover not our blood with your silence." 55. Read "O the Night of Weeping Children" by Nellie Sachs (See ANTHOLOGY) A -What effect did the Holocaust experience have on children and their families? -Interview a child of survivors or one who was a child during the Holocaust to obtain their insight into this question. 56. Study "The Final Solution," (See ANTHOLOGY) BA/A -Respond to the questions in the text. Comment on this quotation from Elie Wiesel's <u>Night</u>, "Man raises himself toward God by the questions he asks Him... that is the true dialogue. Man questions God and God answers. But we don't understand His answers. We can't understand them. Because they come from the depths of the soul, and they stay there until death. You will find only the true answers within yourself."	Many communities have organized "Second Generation" and survivor groups. These may be consulted in conjunction with this activity.
The student will reassess his/her generalizations about human nature in light of the events in Nazi Germany.	"Jewish tradition allows man to say anything to God, provided it be on behalf of man. Man's inner liberation is God's justification. It all depends on where the rebel chooses to stand. From inside his community, he may say everything. Let him step outside of it, and he will be denied this right." 57. Write a report in which you carefully consider the generalizations and/or conclusions which you are able to formulate upon completing this unit. 1. Using the information studied and insights gained in this unit, reevaluate the generalizations about human nature which have developed in previous units. Have your generalizations changed? If so, how? Why? What new evidence can you cite to support your generalizations? Write your responses in preparation for class discussion.	This is an important activity because it emphasizes critical aspects of the inquiry process. Students should be encouraged to provide supports for their generalizations and to recognize that new evidence can either support or reject previous conclusions.

UNIT V: RESISTANCE AND INTERVENTION

INTRODUCTION

In this unit the student will investigate the resistance by
Jews and non-Jews against the Nazis. Often ignored by those who think
they understand the Holocaust, the issue of resistance is crucial to a
proper comprehension of this historical experience. Discussion will focus
on two types of resistance: the more visible open violence of Partisans,
ghetto uprisings, and death camp revolts; and the subtle resistance in the
ghettos and camps.

The unit also focuses upon rescue efforts, apathetic bystanders and
collaborators.

The unit includes a discussion of Erving Goffman's sociological
theory of primary and secondary adjustment; an examination of the attitude
of the Protestant and Catholic churches toward the Holocaust; a review
of those who protested; a survey of the positions of other countries, including the United States, Great Britain, and France; and a study of
theological questions about the place of God in the Holocaust. Focus is
placed upon the moral commitment which should exist among nations and
peoples.

Thus, the unit covers an array of topics and issues through which
the student will examine some of the neglected aspects of the Holocaust
experience.

<u>UNIT GOAL</u>: Although much of the world was reluctant to
become involved, there was local and world-wide Jewish
and non-Jewish resistance.

<u>Performance Objectives</u>:

1. The student will examine the degree of active and passive
    Jewish resistance in the ghettos, forests, and camps.

2. The student will analyze the levels of resistance in
    Germany, in occupied territories, and by the churches.

3. The student will investigate the world response to the
    Holocaust.

4. The student will reassess his/her generalizations about
    the nature of human behavior in light of local and world-
    wide response to the Holocaust.

Anielowicz, Mordecai — A young Jewish resistance leader who died in the Warsaw Ghetto uprising.

Bonhoeffer, Dietrich — The German theologian who decided that Hitler should be assassinated for the moral benefit of the world, and was executed for his role in an unsuccessful attempt on Hitler's life.

Brand, Joel — The Hungarian Zionist active in Jewish rescue efforts.

British White Paper of 1938 — A document which severely limited the immigration of Jews to Palestine.

Christian X — The King of Denmark who refused to release Danish Jews to the Nazis

Concordat — The 1934 agreement between the Vatican and Nazi Germany which neutralized public opposition by the Catholic Church.

Czerniakow, Adam — The chairman of the Warsaw Judenrat who, when learning of the planned deportation, committed suicide.

Evian Conference — The 1938 international conference of Western powers at which the plight of the Jews was discussed. The participating nations refused to make any commitment to receive Jewish refugees.

Gerstein, Kurt — The German officer who protested against the Nazis and ultimately disappeared is described in Rolf Hochhuth's, *The Deputy*.

Klein, Judah — The wigmaker who participated in the famous Treblinka Revolt.

Korczak, Janus — Polish-Jewish educator / doctor who refused to abandon orphans, and thus was sent with them to the Treblinka gas chambers.

Molotov-Ribbentrop Pact of 1939 — The non-aggression pact between Germany and Russia which shocked the world, and set the stage for the German invasion of Poland.

Niemoller, Martin — The German theologian of the Confessional Church who realized too late that failure to protest the persecution of Jews was to accept persecution of all groups.

Pope Pius XII   The Catholic leader whose policy of not making public
                           statements against the Nazis has been the subject of
                           considerable controversy.

Ringelblum, Emanuel   The Warsaw Ghetto historian who buried his works in
                           urns which later were recovered.

Senesh, Hannah   The Haganah parachutist who landed in Nazi-occupied
                           Europe and was executed as a British spy.

St. Louis   The ship containing Jewish emigrants who were refused
                           entry to several countries, including the United States.
                           This "Voyage of the Damned" was eventually sent back
                           to Europe where many of the refugees died.

Stroop, General Jurgen   The German military officer charged with the destruction
                           of the Warsaw Ghetto.

Ten Boom, Corrie   A Dutch Christian who actively hid Jews from Nazi perse-
                           cution, and was later sent to the concentration camp
                           at Ravensbruck. She wrote The Hiding Place.

Vichy Goverment   The interim regime in occupied France which collaborated
                           with the Nazis.

Wannsee Conference   A 1942 meeting in Berlin at which the decision to carry
                           out the Final Solution was made.

Warsaw Ghetto   The first armed resistance against the Nazis in an
       uprising   occupied country, this Jewish uprising was eventually
                           crushed but represented a moral victory.

Weizmann, Chaim   A Zionist leader who encouraged the movement of Jews
                           to Palestine.

Wise, Rabbi Stephen   American Zionist leader who unsuccessfully attempted to get
                           the Roosevelt Administration to intervene in the
                           Holocaust.

UNIT V - UNIT GOAL: Although most of the world was reluctant to become involved, there was some local
and world-wide Jewish and non-Jewish resistance.

PERFORMANCE OBJECTIVES	LEARNING ACTIVITIES/MATERIALS	COMMENTARY

1. The student will examine the degree of active and passive Jewish resistance in the ghettos, forests, and death camps.	1. Read "Torment of a Nation in Chains," and "The Impact of Crisis," in _Stress_, by Ogden Tanner, pp. 106-108, 112-114. A
	  - Explain the diverse reactions of people to the Germans in other occupied countries.
	
	2. Examine the two primary documents, "Appeal of the Jewish Fighting Organization to the Polish Population," and "Samuel Zygelbojm's Last Letter," in _Anthology of Holocaust Literature_," edited by Jacob Glatstein, et al. A
	  - How do you react to the Jewish Fighter's appeal?
	  - Why did Zygelbojm commit suicide?
	
	3. Read three or more of the following on resistance: write a report on the subject.
	
	  a. Read "The Treblinka Revolt," in _Forged in Fury_, by Michael Elkins, pp. 100-119. (See ANTHOLOGY) A
	
	  b. _The War Against the Jews_, by Lucy Dawidowicz A
	    "The Counter Community: The Political Underground," pp. 261-278.
	    "For Your Freedom and Ours," pp. 311-340
	
	  c. "To Die with Dignity," from _Never To Forget_ by Milton Meltzer pp. 137-181 (See ANTHOLOGY) A
	
	  d. _The Holocaust_, by Bea Stadtler, pp. 65-118. BA
	
	  e. _Holocaust and Resistance_, Yad Vashem pamphlet. A
		Please note that ANTHOLOGY refers to THE HOLOCAUST AND GENOCIDE: A SEARCH FOR CONSCIENCE: AN ANTHOLOGY FOR STUDENTS.
		
		The account of the Treblinka Revolt is highly recommended.
		
		Detailed account of resistance in the ghettos.
		
		Excellent written account of specific acts of resistance.
		
		Brief but excellent account of resistance.

PERFORMANCE OBJECTIVES	LEARNING ACTIVITIES/MATERIALS	COMMENTARY

	f. They Fought Back: The Story of the Jewish Resistance in Nazi Europe, by Yuri Suhl. A
	
	   "Little Wanda With the Braids," pp. 51-55
	   "Chief Physician Ramba," pp. 82-84
	   "Mordecai Anielowicz – Commander of the Warsaw Ghetto Uprising," pp. 85-91
		Several short selections which discuss some of the levels of resistance.

	g. Uncle Misha's Partisans, by Yuri Suhl, and "Mottele," by Gertrude Samuels. A	Readable fictionalized accounts of partisan activity.
	h. The Wall, by John Hersey, and "Mila 18," by Leon Uris. A	Fictionalized accounts of Warsaw uprising.
	i. Treblinka, by Jean-Francois Steiner. A	The second half of the book describes the great Treblinka Revolt.
	j. The Survivor, by Terrence Des Pres. A/AA	An outstanding explanation of the different levels of resistance possible in the camps.
	k. A Prayer For Katerina Horovitzova, by Arnost Lustig. BA	Fiction· Expresses the cunning and terror of Brenshe, the German officer.
	l. "The Death of Schillinger" in This Way for the Gas, Ladies and Gentlemen, by Tadeus Borowski, pp. 123-126. AA	This book is depressing in its morbid, detached quality. Schillinger is an SS officer who will meet violent death;a bizarre approach.
	m. Hitler's War Against The Jews, by David Altshuler, pp. 126-141, 150-169. BA	A simplified version of Dawidowicz. Altshuler discusses the counter-community in the ghettos and the Warsaw Ghetto uprising.

4. Read the _Terezin Requiem,_ by Josef Bor.   AA
   Listen to Guiseppe Verdi's "Requiem" which was played by the
   Terezin inmate orchestra. Three sections of the "Requiem"
   were particularly meaningful to the Jewish musicians.

   "Requiem Aeternam" (Grant Eternal Rest)
   "Dies Irae" (Let the day of wrath fall upon those who are
      damned)
   "Libra Me" (Liberate Me)

   —Why would these three sections be meaningful to the musicians?
   —Why did the Germans organize orchestras at the concentration
    camps?
   —Would a performance of the "Requiem" before Adolf Eichmann be
    considered a form of resistance or compliance?

5. Read and discuss, "Resistance in the Camps." (See ANTHOLOGY)
                                                        A

6. Examine the most famous of partisan songs, "Song of the
   Partisans"   (See ANTHOLOGY)   A

    —What was the purpose of this song for resistance fighters?

7. Listen to a speaker who participated in the partisan movement.
   Prepare several key questions for the speaker; summarize
   the exchange in writing.

8. Construct an underground newspaper that might have been
   published in the Warsaw Ghetto.

PERFORMANCE OBJECTIVES	LEARNING ACTIVITIES/MATERIALS	COMMENTARY
	10. In a short essay, respond to the following ethical situation: A young man breaks down when he is told of the death of his family. He decides that in the morning he will commit suicide by attacking an SS officer. Because of the Nazi practice of mass reprisal, his act will cost the lives of the 400 men in his village. All night, the crazed man's comrades try to talk him back to sanity, but his grief is stronger than their appeals. - What should his comrades do with him?	The population of Lidice was destroyed because Reinhardt Heydrich was assassinated by a man from that village.
	11. Respond to "What is the Best Form of Resistance?" (See ANTHOLOGY). A - Are the best forms of resistance always violent?	This activity should inspire a vigorous debate among students about the "real" nature of resistance.
	12. Answer the questions in "Life in Extremis: Moral Action and The Camps" (See ANTHOLOGY) A	The decisions made by camp inmates were never easy. These particular examples demonstrate the "forced choice" nature of an inmate's life.
	13. Read "Revolt in Lachwa" (See ANTHOLOGY) A - What is your reaction to this account?	This selection from Yuri Suhl's They Fought Back, is a good example of collective, almost spontaneous, violent resistance.
2. The student will analyze the levels of resistance in Germany, in occupied territories and by the churches.	1. Read and discuss one or more of the following sources on non-Jewish resistance: a. "Hitler Must Be Killed," in Moral Reasoning, Xerox (AEP) pp. 25-29 A - Would you have supported Bonhoeffer's position? b. Read and respond to "The Ordeal of Dietrich Bonhoeffer; What would you do?" (See ANTHOLOGY) BA/A	Basic explanation of the theologian Bonhoeffer's support of violence against Hitler.

PERFORMANCE OBJECTIVES	LEARNING ACTIVITIES/MATERIALS	COMMENTARY
	b. The Ceremony of Innocence, by James Forman A	Fictional account of German resistance by Hans and Inge Scholl.
	c. The Deputy, by Rolf Hochhuth, pp. 245-256. A - Evaluate the controversy over this play by reading selections from The Storm Over the Deputy by Eric Bentley. A/AA	The Deputy is a very controversial play which is critical of the inaction of Pope Pius XII during the Holocaust.
	d. "The Christian Churches" in Holocaust, by Guenther Lewy and John M. Gnocli, pp. 132-142. A	This selection is the devilish dialogue of Dr. Mengele.
	e. Bright Candles, by Nathaniel Benchley; and Rescue in Denmark, by Harold Flender. A	A novel and a nonfiction work which deal with Danish resistance.
	f. "Teachers and Students," in The Holocaust, by Bea Stadtler (See ANTHOLOGY) BA	
	g. "The Indifferent Ones: In Germany" and "White Rose," in How Democracy Failed, Ellen Switzer, pp. 118-130 (See ANTHOLOGY) BA	
	2. View and discuss at least two of the following films:	
	a. "Joseph Schultz"	A short, sensitive film which presents the heroic refusal of a German soldier to participate in a firing squad execution; based upon an actual incident.
	b. "Silences"	A civilian aids a German soldier but then changes when he sees personal tragedy; beautiful but depressing.

PERFORMANCE OBJECTIVES	LEARNING ACTIVITIES/MATERIALS	COMMENTARY
	c. "Denmark 43"	A recreation of the Danish resistance to the Nazis; excellent film.
	3. Read W. H. Auden's poem, "Joseph Weinheber" A - What is Auden saying in this poem?	
	4. Respond to "The Chemist's Dilemma" (See ANTHOLOGY)	
	5. Play the song, "Crucifixion," by Phil Ochs. - What are the consequences of martyrdom?	This song was written shortly after the assassination of President Kennedy.
	6. Read "The Indifferent Ones: In Hungary" from _The Town Beyond the Wall_, by Elie Wiesel, pp. 160-175 (See ANTHOLOGY) A - How could anyone simply be a spectator to the Holocaust?	A unique meeting between Wiesel and a neighbor who simply _watched_ while the Jews were sent away in trains.
	7. Prepare a bulletin board display in which you illustrate resistance to the Holocaust.	
	8. A great Hasidic master, the Bal Shem Tov, stated, "To pull another out of the mud, a man must step into the mud himself." - Describe an experience where you "stepped in the mud" to help another.	

	9. Comment on the following statements:
	   "The only thing necessary for the triumph of evil is for good men to do nothing." - Edmund Burke
	
	   "If I am not for myself, who will be for me? And if I am for myself alone, who am I ? And if not now - when?" - Hillel
	   - Discuss the relevance of these statements in relation to the issue of non-Jewish resistance and intervention in the Holocaust.	

PERFORMANCE OBJECTIVES	LEARNING ACTIVITIES/MATERIALS	COMMENTARY
	10. Respond to "Anna's Dilemma: What Would You Do?" (See ANTHOLOGY)	
	11. Read "Goodness Incarnate: The People of Le Chambon." (See ANTHOLOGY). A -How do you react to this action? Why do you feel as you do?	This selection is an inspiring story about a French village which quietly resisted the Nazis.
	12. Read "The Church and the Holocaust." (See ANTHOLOGY) A	Historian Gunther Lewy briefly examines the relationship between the Catholic Church and the Third Reich.
	13. Respond to "The Case of Franz Jagerstatter: What Would You Do?" (See ANTHOLOGY) A -Do you consider Jagerstatter's actions courageous or foolish? Why? -Was Jagerstatter acting as a Christian should in the situation?	
	14. Respond to "Lillian Hellman's Dilemma: What Would You Do?" (See ANTHOLOGY)	
	15. Respond to "A Policeman's Dilemma: What Would You Do?" (See ANTHOLOGY)	
3. The student will investigate the world response to the Holocaust.	1. Read at least three of the following; write an essay in which you react to the world response to the Holocaust. a. The Holocaust Years: Society On Trial, "The World Was Silent," edited by Roselle Chartock and Jack Spencer, pp. 151-165. A b. Times of the Holocaust: No Excuse for Apathy, Cleveland Heights High School, Cleveland Heights, Ohio A	This compilation of articles from American periodicals and newspapers raise some disturbing questions.

c. The Politics of Rescue: The Roosevelt Administration and the Holocaust, 1938–1945, by Henry Feingold. "Breckinridge Long," "Perspective on the Roosevelt Administration as Holocaust Witness," pp. 131–137 and pp. 301–307 AA	An interesting figure in the Roosevelt Administration, Feingold offers his sad conclusions.
d. Voyage of the Damned, by Gordon Thomas and Max Morgan Witts. BA	The story of the Saint Louis and its aborted attempt to find a place of refuge for its passengers.
e. "Why Auschwitz Was Never Bombed," by David Wyman, in May 1978, pp. 37–46. AA	Allied failure to bomb the death camps; very disturbing conclusions that the United States simply did not care to bomb Auschwitz.
f. "GM and the Nazis," by Bradford Snell, (See ANTHOLOGY) AA "American Corporations and the Nazis."	
g. "Holocaust Stirs Memories of Switzerland's Epoch of Guilt," in Atlantic City Press, May 13, 1979, p. 12 A (See Appendix)	
h. Read "The Fate of the Hungarian Jews" (See ANTHOLOGY) A —What do you feel was the responsibility of the United States in this situation?	Links major American corporations with the Nazi state.

2. Debate the following: "Resolved: There was nothing the outside world could have done to prevent the Holocaust."

3. Write a play which describes a meeting of Franklin Roosevelt's cabinet in Washington; during the meeting, the cabinet members are to discuss the official American policy toward the Holocaust.

4. When Lord Moyne, British High Commissioner in Egypt in 1944, was told of the possibility of saving one million Hungarian Jews through Eichmann's "Blood for Trucks" deal, he replied, "What shall I do with those million Jews? Where shall I put them?"

PERFORMANCE OBJECTIVES	LEARNING ACTIVITIES/MATERIALS	COMMENTARY
	-How do you react to Moyne's statement? -How might such statements be interpreted by the Germans about the attitude of the world towards their anti-Jewish policy? 5. After the war, Pastor Martin Niemoller of the German Confessing Church is said to have signed the following statement: "In Germany, the Nazis first came for the Communists and I didn't speak up because I wasn't a Communist. Then they came for the Jews, and I did not speak up because I was not a Jew. Then they came for the trade unionists and I didn't speak up because I wasn't a trade unionist. Then they came for the Catholics and I was a Protestant so I didn't speak up. Then they went after the Protestant clergy ... and by then it was too late for anybody to stand up." -Why was there so little early resistance? -What is the responsibility of one person when another citizen is a victim of oppression or injustice? -Describe an experience when you came to the aid of someone who was a 'victim'."	
	6. Construct a series of newspaper headlines or a chart in which you illustrate Jewish efforts to find a new home in various parts of the world prior to implementation of the "Final Solution" in Nazi Germany.	This will show how many nations would not help or provide a home for the Jewish people of Europe.
	7. View the film, "The Hangman" -How does this film relate to the Holocaust?	
4. The student will reassess his/her generalizations about human nature in light of the local and worldwide response to the Holocaust.	1. In this Unit you have analyzed the various ways in which Jews and non-Jews responded to the Holocaust. Given this new information reevaluate your previous generalizations about human nature. Does this new information tend to support or refute your previous views? How? Why? Write your revised generalizations and give supporting evidence.	

UNIT VI: RELATED ISSUES OF CONSCIENCE AND MORAL RESPONSIBILITY

INTRODUCTION

In this unit, the student will relate the moral issues of the
Holocaust to other examples of injustice and oppression, particularly
Afro-Americans, native Americans, and the Vietnamese. The nature of
war and painful questions about our own Vietnam War experience will
be probed. The concept of a war crime will be explored, specifically
in relation to the Nuremberg Trials. The American Civil Rights Movement and the efforts of various groups for social justice will be
studied in an attempt to understand the various strategies for change
and the corresponding difficulties which were encountered.

The student will relate the Holocaust to the modern consciousness;
he/she will thus focus on the central theme of the course, how does
conscience relate to the way we lead our lives? Finally, the student
should see that the struggle for justice is not merely historical,
but one which must play a major role in our daily lives.

<u>Unit Goal</u>: Human beings are confronted by moral dilemmas
and issues of conscience. The Holocaust remains a moral issue
which forces humans to be ever vigilant and alert to destructive
movements which promote anti-human values.

<u>Performance Objectives</u>:

1. The student will analyze the nature of a war crime.

2. The student will examine the legitimacy and impact of the
    Nuremberg War Crimes Trials.

3. The student will determine individual and collective responsi-
    bility for the Holocaust.

4. The student will examine related contemporary issues of
    conscience and moral responsibility.

5. The student will recognize the devastating effects of war.

6. The student will investigate examples of moral decision-
    making in which people have sought, and are seeking, justice
    in their everyday lives.

7. The student will assess the implications of the Holocaust
    for the present and the future, as well as the place of
    conscience in contemporary life.

<u>TERMS</u>

Brown, H. Rap

The "Black Power" advocate who supported the use of violence to win civil rights in the United States during the 1960's.

Calley, Lt. William

The American soldier convicted of responsibility for murdering over 100 civilians at My Lai during the Vietnam War.

defoliation

The American program to destroy the "cover" of the North Vietnamese by stripping the land, burning forests, and destroying vegetation.

Freedom Riders

Northerners who traveled to the South during the 1960's to register Black voters and attempted to further Black racial justice.

Galileo

The Florentine astronomer, physicist, and founder of the science of dynamics, whose support of Copernican ideas led to his condemnation by the Roman Inquisition.

Gandhi, Mahatma

The Indian ascetic who became the spiritual advocate of civil disobedience against British control of his country.

Garrison, William Lloyd

A leading American abolitionist who actively protested against slavery in the United States.

Jackson, Robert

The American prosecutor at the Nuremberg War Crimes Trials.

Jaggerstadter, Franz

An Austrian youth who resisted the German draft, and was subsequently executed.

King, Martin Luther, Jr.

The non-violent American civil rights leader from the 1950's until his assassination in 1968.

More, Sir Thomas

The famous English philosopher, statesmen, and religious leader, who opposed Henry VIII's marriage outside the church, and was beheaded for his "treason" against the state.

Nader, Ralph

The Washington lawyer who serves as consumer advocate.

Nuremberg Trials

The post-World War II trials at which the degree of responsibility of prominent Nazi leaders during the war was determined.

Operation Phoenix

The CIA military program to kill Vietnamese suspected of supporting North Vietnam during the Vietnam War.

pacification	An American military program which was intended to neutralize Vietnamese villages, but which resulted in large scale relocation of the population to major cities, and a greater resentment of Americans.
Rorschach test	The psychological "inkblot" examination used on defendants at Nuremberg.
Socrates	The Greek philosopher accused of impiety and innovation, who chose the punishment of drinking hemlock and dying, rather than illegally leaving the country.
Speer, Albert	Adolf Hitler's minister of armaments who was a defendant at the Nuremberg war crimes trials, and who was sentenced to Spandau Prison.
Stockholm Trials of 1965	The "unofficial" Swedish trials led by Bertrand Russell to assess the responsibility of the American government for war crimes during the Vietnam War.
Thoreau, Henry David	The American philosopher who protested against the Mexican War in 1845, and attempted to draw conclusions about the purpose of life and the responsibility of individuals to themselves.
Wiesenthal, Simon	The famous "Nazi Hunter" responsible for the capture of Adolf Eichmann, who is still searching for Nazi criminals.
Wamashita, Colonel Tomoyuki	The Japanese military leader who was charged with war crimes for atrocities committed by his army in the Philippines during World War II.

UNIT VI – Unit Goal: Human beings are confronted by moral dilemmas and issues of conscience. The Holocaust remains a moral issue which forces humans to be ever vigilant and alert to destructive movements which promote anti-human values.

PERFORMANCE OBJECTIVES	LEARNING ACTIVITIES/MATERIALS	COMMENTARY
		Please note that ANTHOLOGY refers to THE HOLOCAUST AND GENOCIDE: A SEARCH FOR CONSCIENCE, AN ANTHOLOGY.

1. The student will analyze the nature of a war crime.	1. View the filmstrip, "War Crimes."
	  - Compile a list of the issues raised by the viewing. State your opinions about the issues.
	  - Should the Nazis have been prosecuted after World War II?	

	2. Read, "Hitler Before the Seat of Judgment," by Ephraim Lisitsky, in The Voice of My Blood Cries Out, by Murray J. Kohn. A	Hitler speaks on his own behalf in an imaginary trial.
2. The student will examine the legitimacy and impact of the Nuremberg War Crimes Trials.	1. Read one or more of the following selections about the Nuremberg Trials. a. "Judgment at Nuremberg," in The Limits of War, Xerox (AEP) Publication, pp. 13–26 A	Summary of what occurred at the trials.
	b. Forged in Fury, by Michael Elkins, pp. 272–305 A	Blistering indictment of the fact that very few were punished after the war.
	c. The Nuremberg Mind, by Florence Miale and Michael Selzer "Banality," pp. 3–16, "The Mind of the Nazi Leaders," pp. 268–288. AA - Could justice prevail at Nuremberg? Why?	Fascinating analysis of Rhorshach Tests taken by many of the Nuremberg defendants.
	2. Read and react to "The Nuremberg War Crimes Trial." (See ANTHOLOGY) A	

PERFORMANCE OBJECTIVES	LEARNING ACTIVITIES/MATERIALS	COMMENTARY
	3. View the feature film, "Judgment at Nuremberg" - Evaluate the effectiveness of this film.	Maximilian Schell as the defense attorney, Montgomery Clift and Judy Garland as victims. 186 minutes long, but well worth seeing.
	4. Participate in a simulated Nuremberg Trial. Introduction During the Second World War, Germany's enemies and victims gave early warning of their intention to bring war criminals to justice. At the beginning of 1942, nine countries jointly declared that the punishment of war criminals by judicial process was one of their war aims. In November, 1943, Germany's three principal enemies declared that when the war was over, criminals would be handed over to the governments of the countries where their crimes had been committed and that major criminals, whose crimes could not be attached to specific areas, would be tried by an international tribunal. This tribunal, the International Military Tribunal, was formally constituted by an agreement signed in London in 1945 on behalf of the American, British, Russian, and French governments. The principles defined three kinds of crime: crimes against peace, war crimes, and crimes against humanity; and stated that complicity in any such crime was itself a crime under international law. Crimes against peace are defined as planning, preparing, initiating, or waging a war of aggression or a war in violation of international compacts, or participating in a conspiracy to do any of these things. War crimes consist of violations of the customs of war. Examples given include the murder, ill treatment or deportation for slave labor or any other purpose of civilians, the murder or ill treatment of prisoners of war or persons on the seas, killing of hostages, plunder of private property, devastation not	Another fascinating film starring Schell is "The Man in the Glass Booth" which deals with the two themes of guilt and taking responsibility for past behavior.

justified by military necessity. Finally, crimes against
humanity are defined as certain acts against the civilian
population. The acts are: murder, extermination, enslavement,
deportation, inhuman acts, and persecution on political, racial
or religious grounds.

During this simulated Nuremberg Trial, we will try Herman
Goering on these counts. Each person should represent his
person according to historical record. Quotations, statements,
opinions shared by these individuals should be used in the
trial. Evidence (documents, letters, quotations) should be
read to the court by the attorneys. Every student should
keep notes on testimony given in the trial. Time limitations
will be given to respective witnesses and attorneys.

Procedure
- Assume the role of the personality assigned.

- Research the role of the individual assigned; become thoroughly familiar with the views, thoughts, and actions of
  the person. Be thoroughly prepared to answer any questions
  which may be directed by attorneys, members of the press,
  the judge, or other involved parties. Be prepared to offer
  statements relative to your position in the historical events
  and the simulated trial.

- Participate actively in the simulated trial; reflect the
  views and personality of the individual assigned and re-
  searched.

- Submit a written report at the conclusion of the trial. In
  that report, critically assess the reasons for, and outcomes
  of, the Nuremberg Trial.

Day 1 – Assignment of roles
Review of procedures and requirements.

Initial research.

Day 2 – Role research using Media Center, Library, and class-room resources. Discussions with instructor.

Day 3 – Role research continues

Attorneys interview prospective witnesses. Witnesses submit outlines of views and positions to attorneys.

Day 4 – Opening of trial.
Opening statements of the prosecution and defense.

(The duration of the trial will remain flexible and will be determined by the requirements of individual classes.)

Final – Closing statements of prosecution and defense.
Day   Rendering of the verdict by the judge.

Class debriefing and discussion.

Roles

Judge (1)
Attorneys for the Defense (2)
Attorneys for the Prosecution (2)
Court Recorder (1)

Defendant, Herman Goering (Nazi official charged by court with various crimes against humanity, and other specific stated violations.)

Members of the Press (Varying number by class)

Witnesses
(Prosecution)   Elie Wiesel (Survivor)

(Prosecution)   Anne Frank (Tennager who suffered a long ordeal and died at the hands of the Nazis)

PERFORMANCE OBJECTIVES	LEARNING ACTIVITIES/MATERIALS		COMMENTARY
	(Prosecution)	Milton Meltzer (Contemporary authority on anti-Semitism)	
	(Prosecution)	Bernard Malamud (Authority on anti-Semitism; author of The Fixer)	
	(Prosecution)	General George S. Patton (American general; liberator of several concentration/death camps)	
	(Defense)	Gordon Allport (Sociologist; meaning of a scapegoat)	
	(Defense)	Robert Ardrey (Sociologist; aggressive behavior)	
	(Defense)	Rudolph Hoess (Commander of Auschwitz)	
	(Defense)	Albert Speer (Ranking government official under Hitler)	
	(Defense)	Heinrich Himmler (S.S. leader; carried out the "Final Solution")	
	(Defense)	Dr. Mengele (SS. doctor; performed experiments on camp inmates)	
	(Defense)	Joseph Goebbels (Nazi Minister of Propaganda)	
	(Other characters and witnesses may be added in accord with developments in given classes)		
3. The student will determine individual and collective responsibility for the Holocaust.	1. Listen to the song, "Outside a Small Circle of Friends," by Phil Ochs. - How accurate is Ochs' description of our society? - Compare it with Neil Diamond's view in "He Ain't Heavy... He's My Brother."		

PERFORMANCE OBJECTIVES	LEARNING ACTIVITIES/MATERIALS	COMMENTARY

	2. Participate in the exercise "Assessing and Defining Responsibility" (See ANTHOLOGY) A
	
	   - What options were available?
	   - Defend the judgments you were required to make.
	3. Read QB VII, by Leon Uris, pp. 407-421. React to this selection in a discussion. A
		This should result in a provocative dialog over the relative guilt of the individuals.
		
		This selection is from the noted trial of a doctor who helped conduct medical experiments in a death camp.

	4. Many of the corporate executives responsible for policies involving the production of Zyklon B and slave labor received light sentences, and often lived to become very successful businessmen shortly after the war's end.
	   - How does this compare with the way "white collar" crimes are treated in our society?
	   - Why do we find such attitudes towards "white-collar behavior?"	

	5. Listen to the song, "I Never Loved Eva Braun," by the Boomtown Rats (See ANTHOLOGY). - If the singer is the average German citizen, what is this song implying about responsibility for the Holocaust?	This song is highly satiric; the singer states that "he never loved Eva Braun," the German mistress of Hitler.

4. The student will examine related contemporary issues of conscience and moral responsibility	1. Read either The Limits of War, a Xerox (AEP) publication, pp. 34-49; or "Using The Atomic Bomb" from Atomic Diplomacy, by Gar Alperovitz, pp. 236-242; on the decision to drop the atomic bomb on Hiroshima and Nagasaki. (See ANTHOLOGY). A/AA
	   - Participate in a small group discussion in which one-half of the members have read each selection. Based upon your readings, was the decision morally justifiable?
	
	2. View the filmstrip, "Decision to Drop the Bomb: Hiroshima and Nagasaki."
	   - In Truman's place, what would you have done?
		Sets the historical stage for a discussion whether the Truman decision could in any sense be regarded as a "war crime."

PERFORMANCE OBJECTIVES	LEARNING ACTIVITIES/MATERIALS	COMMENTARY
	3. View the film, "Hiroshima/Nagasaki." While the movie is running, play the following songs: "Isn't It About Time," - Stephen Stills "With God On Our Side," - Bob Dylan "Masters of War," - Bob Dylan - Write and discuss immediate reactions to what you have seen and heard.	The juxtaposition of this devastating film with these anti-war songs results in a powerful 17 minutes.
	4. Read one or more of the following selections which focus upon Vietnam:	
	a. Moral Reasoning, Xerox (AEP) Publication; "The Wasting of a Village," pp. 31-35 BA	A simple account, My Lai as a moral issue.
	b. Crimes of War, by Richard Jay Lifton and Gabriel Kolko, "Atrocities in Vietnam" pp. 265-290 AA	An eye-opening analysis of possible American atrocities in Vietnam.
	c. "Nuremberg and Vietnam," by Telford Taylor AA - Relate American Vietnam involvement to the Nuremberg Trials.	Comparison of two historical situations.
	5. View the film, "Interview With My Lai Vets." - React to the way the vets tell their story.	Quickly and passionlessly tells the story of the My Lai slaughter
	6. View "Andersonville," The PBS production of the post-Civil War trial dealing with Southern "war crimes." - In fact, was Captain Henry Wirz guilty of "war crimes?"	This production relates the trial of a southern officer in command of a famous POW camp.
	7. Can corporate leaders be held responsible for committing "immoral" actions? The executives of Krupp, Siemans, and I.G. Farben orporations approved of the ruthless exploitation of starved, overworked camp inmates for the profit of their businesses. They built factories near camps like Auschwitz to save on transportation costs, have access to ample labor and have the gassing facilities to kill their workers when too weak to work. - How would you assess the "ethics" of such people? - Could you describe other examples of exploitation motivated by economics?	

LEARNING ACTIVITIES/MATERIALS	COMMENTARY
3. View the film, "Enemy of the People," a "Sixty Minutes" CBS production. - Should a person working for Lockheed risk his/her job by speaking out about faulty airplanes even if his/her community will be affected? - Explain your point of view.	A comparable situation is explored in Ibsen's play "Enemy of the People."
9. Read "The Trial of Captain Levy " from The Limits of War Xerox (AEP) Publication (See ANTHOLOGY) A - Did Levy have an obligation to train Green Beret medics for Vietnam duty?	
10. In 1961, Adolf Eichmann was kidnapped from Argentina, brought to trial, and executed. Read House on Garibaldi Street, by Harel which describes his capture. See also Justice in Jerusalem, by Hausner which is a report of the trial. A/AA discuss the legitimacy of bringing Eichmann to trial.	
11. Consider the following statement by Creon in the Greek tragedy, Antigone: "The man the state has put in place must have obedient hearing to his least command. When it is right, and even when it's not." - Does this statement justify the obedience of Germans to Nazi policy? - How would this apply in other situations?	
12. Read the following selections from Dissent and Protest, Xerox (AEP) Publication a. "Editor Who Burned the Constitution," pp. 7-8 A b. "Dr. King's Decision in Birmingham," pp. 27-31. (See ANTHOLOGY) A	William Lloyd Garrison's decision to burn the Constitution as a protest against slavery. The beginning of the modern civil rights movement; should motivate a dialogue about the legitimacy of civil disobedience.

PERFORMANCE OBJECTIVES	LEARNING ACTIVITIES/MATERIALS	COMMENTARY
	c. "Militant Who Burned the City," pp. 11–13 A Construct generalizations based upon these three readings.	H. Rap Brown calls for violence.
	13. View the filmstrip, "John Brown; Violence in America" - Did John Brown have the right to use violence?	

	14. View the film, "Black History: Lost, Stolen , or Strayed?"
	
	   - How do you feel about this film?
	
	   - What does it reveal about the impact of film on attitudes of people?
		Classic film narrated by Bill Cosby. Students are not conscious of the manner in which blacks were depicted in early films. The scenes of the teacher instructing his young students in "Black Power" provokes significant reaction.

	15. View the film, "From Montgomery to Memphis." Discuss the moral choices made in the career of Dr. King. - How do you think Dr. King might have responded to the Holocaust?	A good historical portrait of the career of Martin Luther King, Jr. Shows King as a person of conscience and one who held to deep principles for universal justice.
	16. The narrator of "From Montgomery to Memphis" quotes John Donne when he says: "No man is an island, entire of itself; every man is a piece of the continent, a part of the mass; if a cloud be washed away by the sea, Europe is the less, as well as if a promontory were...a man's death diminishes me, because I am involved in mankind, and therefore never send to know for whom the bell tolls; it tolls for thee." - Do you agree?	

	17. Listen to a record of the "I Have A Dream" speech by Martin Luther King, Jr.
	   - How do you react to this speech? Why?
	   - What message does this speech have for us in the 1980's?	

PERFORMANCE OBJECTIVES	LEARNING ACTIVITIES/MATERIALS	COMMENTARY
	18. Read the poem, "Behold the Sea," by Aaron Kurtz (See ANTHOLOGY)A —Compare the experiences of Blacks and Jews.	
	19. Listen to the song, "Only a Pawn in Their Game," by Bob Dylan (See ANTHOLOGY) A —How does Dylan perceive the assassination of Evers? —Do you agree?	The song refers to the assassination of civil rights leader Medgar Evers.
	20. In the 1960's various Black leaders demanded reparations for the oppression of Black people in American history. —Are such victims of oppression entitled in any way to such payment? Why? —Have there been government programs that might be called "reparations?" Elaborate.	
	21. Read "Anniversary for An Unsung Hero," by Cody Shearer (See ANTHOLOGY) A	Evaluate the nature of Jonathan Daniel's sacrifice and his statement about service.
	22. View the film, "Gandhi." Discuss Gandhi's philosophy change.	
	23. View the film, "Lament of the Reservation." Respond to the psychological and physical implications of life on the reservation for the American Indian.	Narrated by Marlon Brando, this is a powerful portrayal of the terrible living conditions and identity problems of reservation Indians today.
	24. Read the screenplay, "Billy Jack," and play the theme from the movie, "One Tin Soldier," by Coven. BA	Billy Jack raises serious questions about the legitimacy of violence in pursuing a just cause.
	25. Read "The Railroad Runs to Canada," from <u>Harriet Tubman</u>, by Ann Petry, pp. 131–138 A — Write an essay in which you evaluate the anti-slavery activities of Harriet Tubman.	Discussion of Harriet Tubman's anti-slavery activities with the Underground Railroad.

PERFORMANCE OBJECTIVES	LEARNING ACTIVITIES/MATERIALS	COMMENTARY
	26. Respond to "Japanese Relocation" (See ANTHOLOGY)	Students should understand the differences between a "relocation center" and a "concentration camp." Nevertheless, the Japanese camps raise some serious ethical issues about the U.S. policy decisions.
	27. View the filmstrip. "Relocation of Japanese Americans: Right or Wrong?" - Respond to the question in writing.	
	28. Read and discuss, "Vietnam and Morality" (See ANTHOLOGY) A	These selections provide an overview of some of the key issues in the Vietnam War from the My Lai massacre to the controversy about Agent Orange.
	29. Examine the chart "Language in Vietnam" (See ANTHOLOGY) - What parallels do you perceive between this language and that of the Nazis?	
	30. Respond to the dilemma, "The Use of Napalm" (See ANTHOLOGY) A	Students should see if there are any parallels between I. G.Farben's production of Zyklon and Dow Chemical's production of Napalm.
	31. Assess the comparability of the events you have studied in this objective in relation to the Holocaust.	

PERFORMANCE OBJECTIVES	LEARNING ACTIVITIES/MATERIALS	COMMENTARY
5. The student will recognize the devastating effects of war.	1. Read "Johnny Got His Gun," by Dalton Trumbo. React to the main character, Joe Bonham, and his suffering. – What is your attitude towards his anti–war feelings?	The horrors of war seen through the eyes of one man who lost all except his power to think, and perhaps to protest against insensitivity.
	2. View the film, "My Country Right or Wrong," from <u>Summertree.</u> – Do you agree with the main character's opposition to being drafted into the Vietnam War?	Raises the issue of draft resistance, and the pressure involved in making such ethical decisions.
	3. Read and react to "Transformation I; From John Wayne to Country Joe and the Fish," in <u>Home From the War,</u> by Robert J. Lifton, pp. 219–27. AA	This section explores the changes in our perception of war as a result of the Vietnam experience.
	4. Read these lyrics from Donovan's "The Universal Soldier"; "He's five foot two and he's six foot four He fights with missiles and with spears He's all of thirty–one and he's only seventeen He's been a soldier for a thousand years... And he knows he shouldn't kill and he knows he always will... And without him all this killing can't go on... And he's fighting for democracy, he's fighting for the Reds He says it's for the peace of all He's the one who must decide who's to live and who's to die, And he never sees the writing on the wall... He's the one who gives his body as a weapon of the war, And without him all this killing can't go on. He's the universal soldier and he really is to blame His orders come from far away no more, They come from here and there, and you and me, and brothers can't you see, This is not the way we put an end to war." – Comment upon this selection. – Is pacifism possible in our world?	

PERFORMANCE OBJECTIVES	LEARNING ACTIVITIES/MATERIALS	COMMENTARY
	5. Read the lyrics to "Where Have All the Flowers Gone?" by Peter Seeger.　　BA 　　- What is Seeger's "Message?"	
	6. Listen to Elton John's "Talking Old Soldiers" 　　- Do you know anyone who has lost close friends or relatives as a result of war? 　　- Reflect on your relationship with them.	
	7. View the feature film, "The Pawnbroker." React to the psychological impact on this survivor of the concentration camps. Does the film have other messages?	The award-winning film about a survivor of the concentration camps who came to New York and lost the capacity to feel compassion.
	8. React to the poem, "Daddy," by Sylvia Plath.	
	9. Read and respond to, "The Survivor," in _Death in Life_, by Robert　Jay Lifton, pp. 479-541　　AA	A comparison of the survivors of Hiroshima and Nagasaki with the death camps.
	10. Based upon what you have studied, is war, or open conflict, ever justified? When? Why?	
6. The student will investigate examples of moral decision-making in which people have sought and are seeking, justice in their everyday lives.	1. Read "The Lawyer Who Jousted With Giants," in _Dissent and Protest_, Xerox (AEP), p. 25-25. A 　Debate: "Resolved: Ralph Nader is a harmful agent in our society, because he does what we should be doing." 　- Discuss the sacrifices involved in assuming the work of a person like Nader.	Focus on the life and work of Ralph Nader.
	2. Research the period of "McCarthyism" in the United States during the late 1940's and early 1950's. Discuss the difficult moral situation which confronted the many people threatened with loss of employment and freedom.	

PERFORMANCE OBJECTIVES	LEARNING ACTIVITIES/MATERIALS	COMMENTARY
	3. View the filmstrip, "Galileo: The Challenge of Reason." - Was Galileo justified in compromising his position with the Church?	Galileo's confrontation with the Church over natural law versus Church doctrine.
	4. View one or more of the following films:	
	a. "The Death of Socrates"	It should be interesting to see whether students are .sympathetic to Socrates' stand, especially his willingness to die.
	b. "A Matter of Conscience"	The bitter confrontation between Henry VIII and Sir Thomas More over the King's unblessed marriage. Will the students accept the principle as one worth dying for?
	c. "Whether To Tell The Truth"	Collection of scenes from "On the Waterfront." Terry Malloy must decide whether to "rat" on his "buddies" for murdering a fellow longshoreman. He pays a price for the stand he takes.
	d. "To See or Not to See"	Humorous cartoon about the decision to see life as it really is, or to create a myth. The illusion works for awhile but eventually leads to the downfall of this sad hero.

PERFORMANCE OBJECTIVES	LEARNING ACTIVITIES/MATERIALS	COMMENTARY

	5. Read "The Myth of Sisyphus," by Albert Camus AA
	
	  - Does Sisyphus' response provide any clue to the effect of the Holocaust or the nature of modern life?
	
	6. View the filmstrip, "Changing the System"
	  - In which options would you participate?
	
	7. Read "The Water Is Wide," by Frank Conroy BA
	
	  - Discuss the value of this type of activity.
	
	8. Read Siddartha, by Herman Hesse AA
	
	  - Comment upon Siddartha's changing way of life.
	
	9. Listen and react to one or more of the following songs:
	
	  a. "The Pretender," by Jackson Browne.
	  b. "The Impossible Dream," from Man of La Mancha
	  c. "My Back Pages," by Bob Dylan
	  d. "We Are Not Helpless," by Stephen Stills (See ANTHOLOGY)
	  e. "Wake Up Everybody," by Gene McFadden, et al. (See ANTHOLOGY)
	  f. "Carry On Wayward Son," by Kansas.
	
	10. Read "A Gradual, Chilling Erosion of Human Values," by Pete Hamill, Philadelphia Inquirer, August 17, 1979. A
	
	  - Discuss the legitimacy of terrorism by the IRA and the British response.
		Presentation of the classic existential tale about a character who tragically exists and strives despite the overwhelming absurdity of his condition.
		
		Story of a compassionate teacher who teaches on an island off South Carolina where the children have had almost no contact with the modern world.
		
		German novel in which one man follows the path of life searching for the meaning of existence and experiences.
		
		These songs should motivate discussion about the possibility of change in our society.

LEARNING ACTIVITIES/MATERIALS

PERFORMANCE OBJECTIVES	LEARNING ACTIVITIES/MATERIALS	COMMENTARY
7. The student will assess the implications of the Holocaust for the present and the future, as well as the place of conscience in contemporary life.	1. Read "Dad, What's a Conscience?" by Marya Mannes, in _Newsweek_, April 15, 1974, p. 11 A – Do you agree with this view of life by a contemporary social critic?	Mannes' critique is a traditional argument; students should understand why.
	2. Read _Brave New World_, by Aldous Huxley. A – Discuss whether the reality of such a future world is possible.	An excellent novel which protests a totalitarian society which brings security without freedom.
	3. Read "The Pull of the Sun Moon," in _New York Times Magazine_, April 30, 1976 AA – Discuss what attracts young people to authoritarian religious movements, and particularly, the Unification Church.	Consider the totalitarian implications and the restriction of freedom placed on the "Moonies."

	4. View the film, "The Sixties."
	   – What were the consequences of this turbulent period of history?
	   – Was it ultimately a "good" or "bad" period?	

	5. Read "Jesus Was No Jew," from _The Racist Reader_, Greenhaven Press, pp. 78-83, and "Rudolf Hess: Prisoner of Peace," pp. 128-135. BA – Discuss the similarity between these recent examples of American right-wing literature and German anti-Semitic materials. Under what circumstances could such American propaganda become effective?	
	6. Read _Wanted: The Search for Nazis in America_, by Howard Blum. – How should we deal with known Nazis living in the United States?	The war criminals issue raises interesting questions about guilt over time, and how long we should "dwell" on atrocities of the past.
	7. View the film, "Judgment at Mineola." – What is your reaction to the attitudes of the citizens of this community?	Originally shown on the CBS program, "Sixty Minutes."

8. Comment on the following statement by Alexander Donat:

   "The Holocaust was the beginning of an era, not its end —
   an era of turmoil and upheaval, of irrationality and mad-
   ness, an era of Auschwitz."

9. Read "Can It Happen Here?" in New York Times Magazine,
   September 20, 1970; and "Adolf Who?" in Time, April 26, 1976. A
   – Discuss the possibility of a type of fascism rising again.
   – Could fascism rise in·the United States?

10. What is "punk rock?" There are some who would argue that the
    recent music phenomenon out of England represents an
    alienated working class movement with fascist leanings.
    Consider the lyrics to the Sex Pistols', "God Save the
    Queen":

        God save the Queen
        A fascist regime
        God..
        Made you a moron
        God..
        She ain't no human being
        And there's no future
        And England's dreaming.

        When there's no future
        How can there be sin?
        We're the flowers in the dustbin
        We're the poison in your human machine
        We're the future
        Your future
        God save the Queen
        We mean it man
        There is no future
        No future for you
        No future for me.
    – What values are represented in these lyrics?
    – Do they inspire optimism or pessimism?

PERFORMANCE OBJECTIVES	LEARNING ACTIVITIES/MATERIALS	COMMENTARY
	11. View the feature film, "Sacco and Vanzetti." - Were they guilty? Prove your case.	An account of the infamous 1920 trial in which two Italian immigrants struggled to clear themselves of a murder/robbery charge.
	12. Read "Holocaust Question" ' by Yehuda Bauer (See ANTHOLOGY) A -Must the Holocaust be viewed as unique to teach valuable lessons? Why?	The recent discussion in the U.S. to build a Holocaust memorial has caused a debate about the relationship of the Holocaust to other genocides.
	13. Read "Pope John Paul at Auschwitz"(See ANTHOLOGY) A -Should a Pope raise issues like the Holocaust even if it might stir painful memories? -What role should organized religion play in the political and social issues of the world?	Pope John Paul's visit to Auschwitz renewed the issue of the place of the church in the affairs of people.
	14. Respond to "Defense of the Rights of the American Nazi Party: A Lawyer's Dilemma" (See ANTHOLOGY) A	The dilemma is a good re-presentation of the contro-versial issue of "Nazi rights."
	15. Read "Sisters of the Third World" (See ANTHOLOGY) A	The issues here range from the recent murders of the politic-ally conscious Maryknoll Sisters in El Salvador to the role of the church in political affairs to the anti-war activities.
	16. Respond to the dilemma "South Africa: University Investment" (See ANTHOLOGY)	The world response to apar-theid in South Africa is a good barometer of the nature of our present decision-making.

PERFORMANCE OBJECTIVES	LEARNING ACTIVITIES/MATERIALS	COMMENTARY
	17. Read "Tyranny in Argentina" (See ANTHOLOGY) A - How do you feel about this situation?	This selection focuses on the experience of Jacobo Timerman in an Argentinian jail.
	18. Read "The Man Who Was Put in a Cage" (See ANTHOLOGY) A - Does this story leave you with hope or despair? Why"	
	19. Read "Letter to Jewish Directors," a Ku Klux Klan letter sent to the Vineland Jewish Community Council, March 2, 1978 BA - React to the letter; write a response.	This is an actual hate letter sent to a Vineland resident after the name appeared in a local newspaper. A copy may be obtained by writing to the Vineland Jewish Community Council, Vineland, New Jersey 08360
	20. Read and discuss, "Tracking the Fiendish Nazi Doctor," by Jack Anderson, in Parade Magazine, November 19, 1978. A	Anderson describes the efforts to find Dr. Mengele.

	21. Read. "The Case of Archbishop Trifa," Time, September 8, 1980, p. 55 A
	
	  - Discuss the arguments for and against the prosecution and extradition of Trifa.
	  - What should be done about him?
		This religious leader, accused of war crimes, is trying to avoid extradition and prosecution.

PERFORMANCE OBJECTIVES	LEARNING ACTIVITIES/MATERIALS	COMMENTARY
	22 . Read, "Accused Nazi War Criminal Leads Quiet Existence," Vineland Times-Journal, March 22, 1980 A - How do you react to this situation?	Karlis Detaus, an accused murderer of Jews, is attempting to silence opposition to his U. S. citizenship removal.
	23.. Read and react to "The Nazi Hunt" (See ANTHOLOGY) A	
	24 . Write an essay in which you evaluate the place of conscience in everyday American life.	
	25 . Prepare a bulletin board which depicts contemporary moral decision-making.	
	26 . Respond to the classic question raised in Dostoevsky's The Brothers Karamazov: "Would you be prepared to torture one small child if you .could end all the sufferings of humanity with this sole act?"	
	27 . Create a work of art which summarizes the feelings you now have about the Holocaust and genocide-related issues.	
	28 . Write an essay in which you explore whether a knowledge of the Holocaust has made you more of an optimist or a pessimist.	
	29 . Discuss the question, "Can there ever be another Holocaust?"	
	30 . Read "Poland Forty Years Later: Where are the Protestors For Poland?" by Richard Cohen; "Jews as Scapegoats" by John Darnton (See ANTHOLOGY) A -What analogies are there between recent events in Poland and the Holocaust? -Why the Jews?	
	31. Read "Heir of the Holocaust: A Child's Lesson" -How does this article relate to the authors "Search for Conscience?"	

BIBLIOGRAPHY

Adler, Jerry, Susan Agrest, and Mary Hager. "Search for an Orange Thread."
    Newsweek, 16 June 1980, p. 56.

    Explores the controversy over Agent Orange and the effects of this
    substance on Americans who served in Vietnam.

Adorno, Theodore. The Authoritarian Personality. N.Y.: Norton, 1969.

    The groundbreaking post-war psychological study of those who are most
    likely to be supportive of Nazi-like thinking. Includes many question-
    naires and interpretation of data.

"After the Massacre." Time, 1 September 1975, pp. 21-22.

    A brief description of atrocities in Bangladesh.

Agar, Herbert. The Saving Remnant. N.Y.: Viking Press, 1960.

    Traces the history of European Jews from the early 20th century to the
    creation of the state of Israel. Excellent chapters about the last years
    of the war and the attempt to save Hungarian Jews.

"Agony of the Boat People." Newsweek. 2 July 1979.

    An overview of the plight of the ethnic Chinese leaving Vietnam.

Allen, William Sheridan. Nazi Seizure of Power: The Experience of a Single
    German Town, 1930-1935. Chicago: Quadrangle, 1965.

    The fascinating account of how Nazism affected the lives of average people
    in a small German town.

Allport, Gordon. ABC's of Scapegoating. N.Y.: Anti-Defamation League of
    B'nai B'rith. Pamphlet.

    An analysis of the various types of scapegoating, with recommendations for
    combatting its growth through education.

Allport, Gordon. The Nature of Prejudice. Abridged, revised edition. N.Y.:
    Doubleday Anchor, 1958. (ADL) Paper.

    A discussion of the roots of prejudice and the role of prejudice in
    history.

Alperowitz, Gar. Atomic Diplomacy: Hiroshima and Potsdam. N.Y.: Vintage
    Books, 1965.

    A different approach to Truman's rationale for the bombing of Hiroshima.

Altshuler, David A. Hitler's War Against the Jews: The Holocaust.
    N.Y.: Behrman House, 1978.

    An excellent history of the Nazi period for young readers. Adapted from
    Lucy Dawidowicz' War Against the Jews.

American Education Publication. <u>Dissent and Protest</u>. Middletown, Conn.: Xerox, 1970.

Case studies of individuals who protested against varieties of social conditions.

American Education Publication. <u>The Limits of War</u>. Middletown, Conn.: Xerox, 1970.

A series of readings and case studies relating to war, war crimes, and international actions.

American Education Publication. <u>Moral Reasoning</u>. Middletown, Conn.: Xerox, 1970.

Provides a brief summary of the Kohlberg theory and a discussion of his stages of moral development. Includes a number of case studies which pose moral dilemmas.

American Education Publication. <u>Nazi Germany</u>. Middletown, Conn.: Xerox, 1969.

Explores the social forces behind the rise of Nazism.

Anderson, Jack. "Ex-Nazi Faces Deportation."

One of the many Anderson columns about Nazis in the U.S. This one concerns Andrija Artukovic, a Yugoslavian accused of war crimes.

Ardrey, Robert. <u>African Genesis</u>. N.Y.: Dell, 1961.

Develops the intriguing and controversial theory that Homo sapiens developed from carnivorous, predatory killer apes, and thus developed an affinity for war.

Arendt, Hannah. <u>The Origins of Totalitarianism</u>. 2nd. rev. ed. Cleveland and N.Y.: World (Meridian Paperbacks), 1958.

A brilliant analysis of the genesis and the nature of Nazi and Stalinist totalitarianism.

Arieti, Sivano. <u>The Will to be Human</u>. N.Y.: Dell, 1972.

An outstanding defense of the view that, although our destiny is not entirely in our hands, we are among the important forces in its creation. Reaffirms the existence of will, freedom, creativity, and originality.

Arlen, Michael. <u>Passage to Ararat</u>. N.Y.: Ballantine, 1975.

An award-winning book which personalizes the fate of the Armenian people and presents the forgotten story of the Armenian Genocide.

Arnold, Eliot. <u>A Kind of Secret Weapon</u>. N.Y.: Scribner, 1969.

The story of ordinary people in Denmark who fight the Nazi's occupation of their homeland.

Auden, W. H. "Joseph Weinheber (1892-1948)," from _In Solitary Witness: Life and Death of Franz Jaggerstatter_. Boston: Beacon Press, 1964.

   The story of an Austrian Catholic peasant executed for refusing to fight in the German Army.

Bar Oni, Bryan. _The Vapro_. Chicago: Visual Impact, Inc., 1976.

   The author tells of her survival as a young Jewish partisan in the Polish forests near her home.

Bauer, Yehuda. _Flight and Rescue: Brichah: The Organized Escape of the Jewish Survivors of Eastern Europe, 1944-1948_. N.Y.: Random House, 1970.

   A documented history of the mass movement of almost 300,000 Jewish survivors by an underground organization.

Bauer, Yehuda. "Holocaust Confusion." _Jewish Exponent_. 11 April 1980.

   An essay which attempts to explain the difference between what happened to Jews in the Holocaust and what has happened to other groups.

Benchley, Nathaniel. _Bright Candles_. N.Y.: Harper and Row, 1974.

   A Danish boy's attempts to help Jewish countrymen. Fiction.

Bentley, Erich, ed. _The Storm Over the Deputy_. N.Y: Grove Press, Inc., 1964.

   A discussion of the controversy begun by the publishing of _The Deputy_ and a reassessment of important documents and information.

Beradt, Charlotte. _The Third Reich of Dreams_. Chicago: Quadrangle, 1968.

   An interesting study of the dreams of those living in Nazi Germany.

Berkovits, Eliezer. _Faith After the Holocaust_. N.Y.: Kiav, 1973.

   Examines the question of retaining religious belief in the face of the horrors of the Holocaust.

Bettelheim, Bruno. _The Informed Heart_. N.Y.: Avon Books, 1971.

   A controversial study of survival and resistance in Nazi camps.

Bettelheim, Bruno. _Surviving_. N.Y.: Alfred A. Knopf, 1979.

   Contains some provocative articles about Eichmann, "the ignored lesson of Anne Frank," and a scathing review of _Seven Beauties_.

Beyer, Barry K. "Conducting Moral Discussions in the Classroom." _Social Education_. April 1976.

   A concise description of a teaching model and teaching strategies for using moral dilemmas in the classroom. The suggestions are related to the research on cognitive-moral development conducted by Lawrence Kohlberg.

Birenbaum, Halina. Hope is the Last to Die. N.Y.: Twayne, 1971.

   A vivid recounting of the author's teenage years in the Warsaw Ghetto,
   Auschwitz, Ravensbruck, and Majdanek, and of her miraculous survival.

Blum, Howard. Wanted: The Search for Nazis in America. N.Y.: Fawcett Crest,
   1977.

   A study of Nazis living in America, and governmental inability to deport
   them.

Bor, Josef. The Terezin Requiem. N.Y.: Avon Books, 1978.

   The story of Raphael Schachter, the Czech conductor, who organized prisoners at Terezin to perform Verdi's Requeim."

Borkin, Joseph. The Crime and Punishment of I. G. Farben. N.Y.: Pocket
   Books, 1978.

   The fascinating account of a German corporation's vital role in Nazi policies, and its conduct at the Nuremberg Trials.

Borowski, Tadeusz. This Wy to the Gas, Ladies and Gentlemen and Other
   Stories. Translated from the Polish. N.Y.: Viking Press, 1967.

   A powerful collection of short stories depicting the horrors of Auschwitz.

Bosch, William. Judgment on Nuremberg. Chapel Hill: University of North
   Carolina Press, 1970.

   Examines the attitudes of Americans toward the famous war crimes trials.

Bosworth, Allen R. America's Concentration Camps. N.Y.: W. W. Norton, 1967.

   An evaluation of the internment of Japanese-Americans during World War II,
   and a discussion of the issues relating to this action.

Boyajian, Dickran H. Armenia: The Case for a Forgotten Genocide. Westwood,
   N.J.: Educational Book Crafters, 1972.

   Discusses the events leading to genocide in Turkey.

Brown, Dee. Bury My Heart at Wounded Knee: An Indian History of the American
   West. N.Y.: Bantam Books, 1974.

   A controversial history of the destruction of the American Indians and
   their relationship to the rest of America.

Bullock, Alan. Hitler: A Study in Tyranny. N.Y.: Harper and Row, 1964.

   A traditional biography of Hitler.

Calley, William. Lieutenant Calley. N.Y.: Grosset and Dunlap, 1971.

   Presents Calley's account of his tour in Vietnam, the My Lai massacre, and
   the subsequent court martial.

"Cambodia: An Experiment in Genocide." *Time*, 31 July 1978, pp. 39-40.

   An essay which raises questions about the larger meaning of atrocities in
   Cambodia.

Camus, Albert. *The Myth of Sisyphus*. N.Y.: Vintage, 1955.

   A collection of philosophical essays which analyze the absurdity of human
   life.

Camus, Albert. *The Plague*. N.Y.: Alfred A. Knopf, 1966.

   One of the most important novels of the post-war era. An allegory which
   suggests the French resistance movement by telling the story of a plague
   and those who fight it.

Caputo, Philip. *A Rumor of War*. N.Y.: Holt, Rinehart and Winston, 1977.

   A novel written by a Vietnam veteran which demonstrates the effects of the
   war on the behavior of American soldiers. Basis of a television movie.

Cassou, Jean. *Chagall*. N.Y.: Praeger Publishing, 1965.

   An overview of the artistic career of one of the most important modern
   Jewish artists.

Chaneles, Sol. *Three Children of the Holocaust*. N.Y.: Avon Books, 1975.

   A novel about three Auschwitz survivors and their adjustment to adoption in
   America.

Chartock, Roselle and Spencer, Jack, eds. *The Holocaust Years: Society on
   Trial*. N.Y.: Bantam, 1978.

   A collection of readings on the Holocaust.

Chrakian, Elisha B. *Vital Issues in Modern Armenian History*. Watertown,
   Mass.: Armenian Studies, 1965.

   A series of essays about the genocide of the Armenian people in Turkey.

Cohen, Elie A. *Human Behavior in the Concentration Camp*. (trans. from the
   Dutch) N.Y.: Grosset and Dunlap (Universal Library Paperback), 1953.

   A Jewish psychiatrist survivor's valuable study of camp society at
   Auschwitz and Mauthausen.

Cohen, John, ed. *The Essential Lenny Bruce*. N.Y.: Ballantine Books, 1967.

   A compilation of some of the best comic material by this controversial
   satirist, including "My Name is Adolf Eichmann."

Cohn, Norman. "The Myth of the Jewish World Conspiracy," *Commentary*, June
   1966.

   Traces the rise of *The Protocols of the Elders of Zion*, and explores the
   psychological motivation for anti-Semitism.

Cohn, Norman. <u>Warrant for Genocide</u>. N.Y.: Harper and Row, 1969. (ADL)

   Traces the growth of the mythology of modern anti-Semitism.

Conrat, Maisie and Richard. <u>Executive Order 9066</u>. San Francisco: California
   Historical Society, 1972.

   A photo essay including authentic scenes of American concentration camp
   experiences.

Conroy, Frank. <u>The Water is Wide</u>. N.Y.: Dell, 1972.

   An autobiographical account of the author's attempt to teach southern Black
   children in the midst of an atmosphere of racism and indifference.

Conway, John S. <u>The Nazi Persecution of the Churches, 1933-45</u>. N.Y.: Basic
   Books, 1968.

   A scholarly account of the reaction of the German Protestant and Catholic
   churches to Nazism.

Cook, Joan Marble. <u>In Defense of Homo Sapiens</u>. N.Y.: Dell, 1975.

   Sharply disagrees with the Ardrey-Lorenz theories. The author offers new
   documentation to support the view that human self-esteem is essential to
   the dignity of man.

Daniels, Roger. <u>Concentration Camps U.S.A.: Japanese Americans and World War
   II</u>. N.Y.: Holt, Rinehart and Winston, 1972.

   A detailed study of the personalities and conditions that caused the
   internment of Japanese-Americans.

Dawidowicz, Lucy S., ed. <u>The Golden Tradition: Jewish Life and Thought in
   Eastern Europe</u>. N.Y.: Holt, Rinehart and Winston, 1967.

   An excellent anthology presenting the works of Eastern European Jews from
   the late 19th to the early 20th century.

Dawidowicz, Lucy, ed. <u>A Holocaust Reader</u>. N.Y.: Behrman House, 1976.

   Selections of Nazi related and Jewish records which parallel the author's
   <u>The War Against the Jews</u>.

Dawidowicz, Lucy. <u>The War Against the Jews, 1933-1945</u>. N.Y.: Holt, Rinehart
   and Winston, 1975. Bantam, 1976. Paper.

   A detailed account of Nazi actions directed against the Jews of Eastern
   Europe from 1933-1945.

Delbo, Charlotte. _None of Us Will Return_. Boston: Beacon Press, 1968.

   One woman's struggle for survival in a death camp. Poetic.

Deloria, Jr., Vine. _Behind the Trail of Broken Tears_. N.Y.: Delta Books, 1974.

   A highly critical account of the Bureau of Indian affairs and its vain attempt to deal with Indian problems.

Deloria, Jr., Vine. _Custer Died for Your Sins: An Indian Manifesto_. N.Y.: Avon Books, 1975.

   This eye-opener dispels the persistent stereotypes and historical inaccuracies concerning the Native Americans.

Des Pres, Terrence. _The Survivor: An Anatomy of Life in the Death Camps_. N.Y.: Oxford University Press, 1976.

   A stark account of the struggle for survival in concentration camps and the factors contributing to this survival.

Dimensions of the Holocaust. Evanston, Ill.: Northwestern Univ., 1977. (ADL)

   A collection of several speeches given at this mid-western university by Holocaust authorities, including Elie Wiesel.

Donat, Alexander. _The Holocaust Kingdom: A Memor_. N.Y.: Holt, Rinehart and Winston, 1965. Schocken Books, 1978. Paper. (ADL)

   A first-hand account which concentrates on ghetto and camp life.

Dostoevsky, Fyodor. _The Brothers Karamazov_. N.Y.: Bantam Books, 1974.

   Classic Russian novel which gives major insight into human nature.

Duffett, John, ed. _Against the Crimes of Silence_. N.Y.: Simon and Schuster, 1970.

   An excellent collection of evidence used at the unofficial Stockholm War Crimes Trial which judged the "war guilt" of the United States in Vietnam.

Eckardt, A. Roy. _Your People, My People_. N.Y.: Quadrangle, 1974

   Deals with relationships between Christians and Jews. Especially concerns the relationship between anti-Semitism and Christian teaching.

Ehrlich, Annette. "The Adaptable Primates." _Human Behavior_, November 1976. pp. 25-30.

   Makes a good case for the diversity in animal behavior and the danger in comparing human with animal behavior.

"18% Call Nazi Era the Good Old Days." Philadelphia Inquirer, 17 March 1981.

A news article which states the results of a Der Spiegel survey about contemporary Germans' views of the past.

Elkins, Michael. Forged in Fury. N.Y.: Ballantine, 1971. Paper.

Stories of Holocaust survivors who formed a secret organization to avenge the deaths of Jews.

Elson, Robert T. Prelude to War. N.Y.: Time-Life Books, 1977.

An illustrated source which documents the years from the end of World War I through the rise of Hitler.

Englebardt, Stanley 1. "Bus of Quiet Terror." Reader's Digest, September 1979, pp. 20-4.

The heroic story of several citizens who came to the rescue of an overturned school bus containing deaf children.

Epstein, Leslie. King of the Jews. N.Y.: Coward, McCann and Geoghegen.

A disturbingnovelwhich treats the subject of the Judenrat. It is questionable whether the novel really captures the behavior and motives of Judenrat members.

Erasmus and Otto Dix. Bellum. Barre, Mass.: Imprint Society, 1972.

Completed after World War I, the text includes some extraordinary drawings by Dix.

Evans, Richard I. "Whispers of Nazi: The Short Political Aberration of Konrad Lorenz." Psychology Today, November 1974, pp. 84-5.

Interesting information about Lorenz' early years in Nazi Germany.

Falk, Richard A., Gabriel Kolko, and Robert Jay Lifton, eds. Crimes of War. N.Y.: Vintage, 1971.

An inquiry into the nature of criminal acts in wars. Includes some excellent selections about Vietnam, and probes the controversial comparison with Nazi atrocities.

Fein, Helen. Accounting for Genocide. N.Y.: The Free Press, 1979.

Analysis of the extent of participation of different countries in the Holocaust process.

Feingold, Henry L. The Politics of Rescue: The Roosevelt Administration and the Holocaust, 1938-1945. New Brunswick: Rutgers University Press, 1970.

A detailed account of the failure of U.S. foreign policies to deal with the realities of the Holocaust.

Feldstein, Stanley. <u>The Poisoned Tongue</u>. N.Y.: William Morrow, 1972.

A documentary history about various types of racist and anti-Semitic literature.

Fenelon, Fania. <u>Playing for Time</u>. N.Y.: Atheneum, 1977.

Memoir about a French Jewish singer's experience in Auschwitz as a member of the orchestra. Recently a controversial television movie starring Vanessa Redgrave.

Fenton, Edwin. "Moral Education: The Research Findings." <u>Social Education</u>, April 1976.

Reviews the major research findings on cognitive-moral development which resulted from the work of Lawrence Kohlberg. Implications for social studies instruction are discussed.

Fest, Joachim C. <u>The Face of the Third Reich</u>. N.Y.: Pantheon Books, 1970.

Written by one of the best contemporary German historians. Discusses the careers of many leading Nazis.

Finkelstein, Milton, et al. <u>Minorities. U.S.A</u>. N.Y.: Globe Book Co.

A view of the role of minorities in America.

Fleischner, Eva, ed. <u>Auschwitz: Beginning a New Era? Reflections on the Holocaust</u>. N.Y.: ADL. 1977. Paper.

Discusses the Holocaust, discrimination today, Christian education, Blacks and Jews, and art and culture after the Holocaust.

Flender, Harold. <u>Rescue in Denmark</u>. N.Y.: MacFadden, 1964. (ADL) Paper.

A description of the effort of the Danish people to save Jews in 1943.

Flinker, Moshe. <u>Young Moshe's Diary: The Spiritual Torment of a Jewish Boy in Nazi Europe</u>. Jerusalem and N.Y.: Board of Jewish Education, 1965.

The impact of Nazi policy as seen through the eyes of a religious boy from Holland.

Forman, James. <u>Ceremony of Innocence</u>. N.Y.: Hawthorne, 1970.

Fiction based upon fact abut a Christian brother and sister who pay with their lives for publishing "The White Rose," leaflets which denounced the Nazis.

Forman, James D. <u>The Survivor</u>. N.Y.: Farrar, Straus, and Giroux, 1976.

A powerful novel about a prosperous Amsterdam clan and its gradual disintegration under the Nazis. Ends with the survival of just one member.

Forsyth, Frederick. The Biafra Story. Baltimore: Penguin Books, 1969.

A good overview and explanation of events and circumstances leading up to and including the Biafran struggle for independence.

Forsyth, Frederick. _The Odessa File_. N.Y.: Bantam, 1974.

   A fictional account of one man's search for a Nazi war criminal, and his
   surprising motive for that search.

Fortney, Alan Jay. _Could You KIll?_ N.Y.: Harper and Row, 1973.

   Clearly discusses the various _schools of thought about the origins of human
   behavior.

Fraenkel, Jack R., ed. _Prejudice and Discrimination_. Englewood Cliffs;
   Prentice Hall, 1977.

   Examines contemporary issues on prejudice and discrimination through
   selected articles.

Frank, Anne. _Diary of a Young Girl_. N.Y.: Pocket Books, 1953. Paper.

   The new classic account of a young Jewish girl hiding from the Nazis in
   Amsterdam.

Frank, Anne. _The World of Anne Frank_. Conn.: Greenwood, 1974.

   The contents of two notebooks Anne Frank left behind when arrested by the
   Dutch Nazi police. Includes the diary, essays, stories, and reminiscences
   of her earlier life in Amsterdam.

Frankl, Victor. _Man's Search for Meaning: An Introduction to Logotherapy_.
   Boston: Beacon Press, 1963. Pocket Books. Paper.

   A first-hand account of experiences in Auschwitz, concentrating on the
   finding of meaning in life through suffering.

Friedlander, Saul. _Kurt Gerstein: The Ambiguity of Good_. N.Y.: Alfred A.
   Knopf, 1969.

   Discusses the life of Kurt Gerstein, the Catholic Nazi, who had first-hand
   knowledge of both the "euthanasia" program and the Balzac gas chambers. He
   would eventually go to the Pope for aid.

Friedlander, Albert H., ed. _Out of the Whirwind: A Reader of Holocaust
   Literature_. N.Y.: Union of American Hebrew Congregation, 1968. Paper.

   Excerpts from novels, memoirs, diaries, and short stories depicting
   Holocaust-related experiences.

Friedman, Philip. _Martyrs and Fighters: The Epic of the Warsaw Ghetto_. N.Y.:
   Praeger, 1954.

   An excellent account of the Warsaw Ghetto experience from beginning to end.

Friedman, Philip. _Their Brothers' Keepers: The Christian Heroes and Heroines
   Who Helped the Oppressed Escape the Nazi Terror_. N.Y: Crown, 1957. (ADL)

   A comprehensive record of individuals and church groups which helped Jews
   in danger.

Fromm, Erich.   The Anatomy of Human Destructiveness.   Greenwich: Fawcett,
    1973.

    Discusses the haunting problem of people's propensity for cruelty.

Fromm, Erich.   Escape From Freedom.   N.Y.: Holt, Rinehart and Winston, 1941.
    Avon, 1971.   Paper.

    According to the author, if a person cannot stand freedom, he or she will
    probably turn Fascist.

Furman, Harry, Ed.-in-Chief, eds.   The Holocaust and Genocide: A Search for
    Conscience, An Anthology.   N.Y.: Anti-Defamation League of B'nai B'rith,
    1982.

    A collection of readings, educational activities, and moral dilemmas which
    focus on all aspects of the Holocaust, as well as genocide in general.

Galbraith, Ronald and Thomas Jones.   Moral Reasoning.   MN: Greenhaven Press,
    1976.

    Based on psychologist Lawrence Kohlberg's theory of cognitive-moral devel-
    opment.   Applicable for both secondary and elementary school teachers.

"Genes Uber Alles."   Time.   13 December 1976.   pp. 93-4.

    The basic beliefs of the socio-biological school of thought.

Gersten, Irene, and Betty Bliss.   Ecidujerp, Prejudice.   N.Y.: Franklin Watts,
    Inc., 1974.

    A simple book about the origins of and motivations for prejudice.   Also
    discusses ways of dealing with prejudice.

Gilbert, G. M.   Nuremberg Diary.   N.Y.: Farrar, Straus, Giroux, 1947.   Signet,
    1961.   Paper.

    A discussion of the Nuremberg Trials, including interviews with both
    prisoners and prosecutors.

Gilbert, Martin.   Final Journey.   N.Y.: Mayflower Books, 1979.

    A good discussion of the fate of Jews in various European communities.

Gilbert, Martin.   The Holocaust.   N.Y.: Hill and Wang, 1978.

    An excellent compilation of maps, photographs, and commentary on the
    Holocaust.

Ginott, Haim.   Teacher and Child.   N.Y.: MacMillan, 1972.

    Discusses teacher-student relationships, and includes a letter from Ginott,
    a survivor, to teachers.

Glatstein, Jacob, ed.   Anthology of Holocaust Literature.   Phila.: Jewish
    Publication Society, 1977.

    Writings by eyewitnesses and survivors.

Golding, William. _Lord of the Flies_. N.Y.: G.P. Putnam, 1954.

   The classic novel of young boys' descent into evil while stranded on an
   island.

Gornick, Vivian and Moran, Barbara, eds. _Woman in Sexist Society_. NY: Basic
   Books, 1971.

   A feminist anthology of readings concerning the condition of women in
   Western culture.

Graber, G.S. _The History of the S.S._ Grosset and Dunlap, 1978.

   An account of the background of and rationale behind the S.S.

Grant, Jonathan. _Cambodia: The Widening War in Indochina_. N.Y.: Washington
   Square Press, 1971.

   Articles by Noam Chomsky and Jean Lacoutre which examine the effects of
   saturation bombing, genocide, forced urbanization, and other issues.

Green, Gerald. _Holocaust_. N.Y.: Bantam Books. 1978.

   Novel of a Jewish physician and his family from 1935 to 1945 as they are
   brutalized by the Nazis. Based on the television series.

Grunberger, Richard. _Hitler's S.S._ N.Y.: Dell, 1971. Paper.

   A detailed account of the background, psychology, and practices of the S.S.

Grunberger, Richard. _Twelve Year Reich: A Social History of Nazi Germany,
   1933-1945_. N.Y.: Holt, Rinehart and Winston, 1971.

   A valuable accunt of Nazi society and life during the Third Reich.

Grunfeld, Frederic F. _The Hitler File: A Social History of Germany and the
   Nazi 1918-4_. N.Y.: Random House, 1974.

   A photo account of Nazi society and culture.

Grynberg, Henryk. _Child of the Shadows, Including the Grave_. London:
   Valentine, Mitchell, 1969.

   An autogiographical account of a child's attempt to deal with life and
   death in the Warsaw underground.

Hallie, Philip P. _Lest Innocent Blood Be Shed_. N.Y.: Harper and Row, 1979.

   An inspiring account of the efforts of the people of Le Chambon, France, to
   rescue Jews from Nazi murder.

Hamill, Pete. "A Gradual Chilling Erosion of Human Values." _Philadelphia
   Inquirer_, 17 August 1979.

   A dramatic account of the horror of urban warfare in Northern Ireland, and
   of one man's protest.

Hammer, Richard. <u>One Morning in the War</u>. N.Y.: Coward McCann, 1970.

A chilling account of the savagery of the Son MY massacre in Vietnam.

Haeger, Heinz. <u>The Man with the Pink Triangle</u>. Boston: Alyson Publications,
1980.

The experience of homosexuals in the concentration camps.

Hersey, John. <u>The Wall</u>. N.Y.: Bantam, 1950.

A monumental novel about the creation of the Warsaw Ghetto, and about life
and revolt within its walls.

Harsh, Seymour. <u>Cover Up!</u> N.Y.: Random House, 1972.

Based on official transcripts of the military investigation of the My Lai
massacre. Focuses on the morality of war, genocide, and loyalty.

Hess, Hans. <u>George Grosz</u>. N.Y.: MacMillan Publishing Co., 1974.

An illustrated analysis of the work of the famous Weimar artist and critic.

Hilberg, Raul. <u>The Destruction of the European Jews</u>. Chicago: Quadrangle,
1961. New Viewpoints, 1973. Paper.

A masterful scholarly account of the planning and execution of the Nazi
program for destruction.

Hillel, Marc, and Clarissa Henry. <u>Of Pure Blood</u>. N.Y.: McGraw-Hill, 1976.

An account of the Nazi Lebensborn program, the attempt to develop a master
race by breeding.

Hinz, Berthold. <u>Art in the Third Reich</u>. N.Y.: Pantheon Books, 1979.

A study of Nazi art, complete with many pages of illustrations.

Hochhuth, Rolf. <u>The Deputy</u>. N.Y.: Grove Press, 1964. Paper.

The controversial play about the role of Pope Pius XII during the
Holocaust.

Hoffer, Eric. <u>The True Believer</u>. N.Y.: Harper and Row, 1951.

Examines the psychology of mass movements and those who join them.

Hohne, Heinz. <u>The Order of the Death's Head</u>. N.Y.: Ballantine Books, 1977.

An excellent account of the origins of the S.S., and the activities of
horror in which they engaged.

<u>Holocaust</u>. Jerusalem: Keter. Distributed by ADL, 1974. Paper.

Section on history, behavior of the victims, the camps, Hitler, partisans,
rescues, Christian Churches, war crimes, Eichmann trial, Arab attitudes,
Soviet Union, historiography.

<u>The Holocaust and Resistance</u>. Yad Vashem, Israel, 1972.

    A pamhlet which presents an overview of the Holocaust. Striking photos.

Housepian, Marjorie. <u>The Smyrna Affair</u>. N.Y.: Harcourt, Brace, Jovanovich,
    1971.

    An account of the brutal massacre of Armenians by the Turks during World
    War I.

Houston, Jeanne Wakatsuki, and James. <u>Farewell to Manzanar</u>. N.Y.: Bantam
    Books, 1973.

    The story of Jeanne Wakatsuki's family four years in an internment camp.

Howard, Ted, and Jeremy Rifkin. <u>Who Should Play God?</u> N.Y.: Dell Publishing
    Co., 1977.

    One of the first books to deal with the possible consequences of recent
    life-creating technology on future society.

Hull, David Stewart. <u>Film for the Third Reich</u>. N.Y.: Simon and Schuster,
    1979.

    A thorough account of the use of film and the acting community as instru-
    ments of propaganda in Nazi Germany.

Huxley, Aldous. <u>Brave New World</u>. N.Y.: Harper and Row, 1969. Paper.

    Novel that explores a vision of the future involving centralized control.

Hyams, Joseph. <u>A Field of Buttercups</u>. N.J.: Prentice-Hall, 1968.

    Novel about the renowned Jewish Polish physician-educator Janusz Korczak,
    who chose to go to death with 200 children of his "Our Home" orphanage
    despite the opportunity to save himself.

Isherwood, Christopher. <u>Berlin Stories</u>. N.Y.: New Directions, 1954. Paper.

    Short stories on which the film <u>Cabaret</u> is based.

Ishigo, Estelle. <u>Lone Heart Mountain</u>. Los Angeles: Estelle Ishigo, 1972.

    A discussion of the evacuation of Japanese-Americans after Executive Order
    #9066.

Ish-Kisher, Sulamith. <u>A Boy of Old Prague</u>. N.Y.: Pantheon Books, 1963.

    An excellent juvenile novel about a young boy in Prague in 1540, and what
    he learns about Jews and prejudice.

Jones, Ron. "You Will Do As Directed." <u>Learning</u>, May 1975.

    An account of a social studies teacher's experiment in authoritarianism,
    and its frightening results.

Jordon, Winthrop. White Over Black. Baltimore: Penguin Books, 1968.

   This monumental work explores the origins and evelopment of white attitudes
   toward Blacks from the sixteenth century to the early years of the
   Republic.

Kahler, Erich. The Tower and the Abyss. N.Y.: George Braziller, Inc., 1957.
   A classic study of the growing alienation and decay characterizing the
   twentieth century.

Kanfer, Stefan. The Eighth Sin. N.Y.: Random House, 1978.

   A novel about a young Gypsy which emphasizes the murder of his family in
   the Holocaust.

Kantor, Alfred. The Book of Alfred Kantor. N.Y.: McGraw Hill, 1971.

   The artist's work done while a prisoner at Terezin and Auschwitz.

Kampowski, Walter. Did You Ever See Hitler? N.Y.: Avon Books, 1975.

   Five hundred interviews with people who lived under Hitler's rule.

Kinelman, Donald. "A Quiet Man, A Suspect Past." Philadelphia Inquirer, 14
   July 1980.

   A news article about a man in Philadelphia who is now suspected of having
   been a Nazi war criminal.

Kinsar, Bill, and Neil Kleinman. The Dream That Was No More a Dream. N.Y.:
   Harper and Row, 1969.

   A highly creative book which links Nazi Germany to German culture. Many
   paintings, posters, and cartoons are included.

Klein, Gerda Weissman. All But My Life. N.Y.: Hill and Wang, 1971.

   A moving autobiographical account of a woman who spent her late teens as a
   slave laborer for the Nazis.

Klein, Mina and H. Arthur. Kathe Kollwitz. N.Y.: Schocken Books, 1975.

   A good discussion of the life and work of the famous German artist who was
   persona non grata in the Third Reich.

Koehn, Ilse. Mischling, Second Degree. N.Y.: William Morrow, 1977.

   An account of a young girl of mixed heritage growing up in Nazi Germany.

Kohn, Murray J. The Voice of my Blood Cries Out. N.Y.: Shengold Publishers,
   1979.

   A study of predominant Holocaust themes as reflected in Yiddish and Hebrew
   poetry during and after the Holocaust.

Komorowski, E.A. with Gilmore, Joseph L. *Night Never Ending*. N.Y.: Avon
    Books, 1974.

    The story of the massacre of Poles in the Katyn Forest, and a survivor's
    fight for normalcy.

Kosinski, Jerzy. *The Painted Bird*. Boston: Houghton Mifflin, 1965. N.Y.:
    Bantam, 1972. Paper.

    A novel about a young boy's terrible adventures among superstitious
    peasants in Eastern Europe during the war.

Kracauer, Siegfried. *From Caligari to Hitler*. Princeton, N.J.: Princeton
    University Press, 1947.

    Presents the thesis that the German films of the twenties were filled with
    premonitions of the totalitarionism of the thirties, and that Hitler arose
    as the resolution of psychological dilemmas reflected in these films.

Kraus, Ota, and Erich Kulka. *The Death Factor*. N.Y.: Pergamon Press, 1966.

    An excellent review of life in the death camps.

Kroll, Erwin, and Judith Nies McFadden, ed., *War Crimes and the Ameican
    Conscience*. N.Y.: Holt, Rinehart and Winston, 1970.

    A collection of essays and discussions which integrate the Vietnam War
    issue into the larger debate regarding what constitutes "genocide" or "war
    crimes."

Kuznetsov, Anatoli. *Babi Yar: A Documentary Novel*. Uncensored edition.
    N.Y.: Farrar, Straus, Giroux, 1970. Censored edition. N.Y.: Dell, 1967.
    Paper.

    A Russian boy's view of the massacre of Jews at Babi Yar.

Lambert, Gilles. *Operation Hazalah*. N.Y.: Bobbs-Merrill, 1974.

    Young Zionists enable thousands of Hungarian Jews to escape massacre in the
    closing days of the war.

Langer, Walter. *The Mind of Adolf Hitler*. N.Y.: Signet Books, 1972.

    The first psychological profile of Hitler, commissioned by the U.S. Intel-
    ligence Service in the 1940's.

Laqueur, Walter. *The Terrible Secret*. Boston: Little, Brown, 1980.

    An excellent discussion of the extent of knowledge throughout the world
    about the death camps.

Leakey, Richard, and Roger Lewin. "Is It Our Culture, Not Our Genes, That
    Makes Us Killers?" *Smithsonian*, November, 1974, pp. 36-44.

    Defends the thesis that environment, not genes, influence our behavior.

Leakey, Richard E., and Roger Lewin. People of the Lake. N.Y.: Avon, 1978.

    A counter-argument to the man-as-killer theory. The authors believe that
    man survived because of his cooperative efforts, rather than his aggres-
    siveness.

Leary, Mike. "The Nazi Hunt: One Case." The Philadelphia Inquirer,
    24 October 1976.

    A journalistic account of a Rumanian bishop's attempts to escape deporta-
    tion in order to stand trial for his leadership in the Rumanian Iron Guard,
    a group responsible for the deaths of thousands.

Leitner, Isabella. Fragments of Isabella. N.Y.: Dell, 1978.

    A memoir about the author's experiences at Auschwitz.

Lengyel, Emil. Turkey. N.Y.: Random House, 1941.

    A documented history of Turkey which gives good insight into the tragedy of
    the Armenian people while they lived in that country.

Lengyel, Olga. Five Chimneys: The Story of Auschwitz. N.Y: Ziff-Davis, 1947.

    A strong account of one woman's experience in the death camps. A section
    deals with "scientific" experiments.

Levi, Primo. Survival in Auschwitz. N.Y.: Collier, 1958.

    The Italian chemist's personal account of his experience in that infamous
    camp.

Levin, Nora. The Holocaust: The Destruction of European Jewry, 1933-45.
    N.Y.: Crowell, 1968.

    Excellent full reference work on the Holocaust.

Levitin, Sonia. Journey to America. N.Y.: Atheneum, 1973.

    A fictional account of one German family's decision to leave home for the
    safety of America, and the experiences encountered as a result of this
    decision.

Lieberman, Herbert. The Climate of Hell. N.Y.: Pocket Books, 1978.

    A novel which includes some discussion of Dr. Josef Mengele, and of the
    destruction of the Ache Indians in Paraguay.

Lifton, Robert Jay. Death in Life. N.Y.: Simon and Schuster, 1967.

    A brilliant book which explores the effects of the bombing of Hirochima and
    Nagasaki on Japanese survivors.

Lindner, Robert. The Fifty Minute Hour. N.Y.: Bantam, 1973.

    A series of five psychological case studies, including a psychological
    portrait of an American Nazi during the war.

Lowenstein, Rudolph M. Christians and Jews. N.Y.: Dell, 1951.

    Primarily a psychological analysis of the causes and effects of
anti-Semitism.

Lustig, Arnost. A Prayer for Katerina Horovitzova. N.Y.: Avon Books, 1973.

    A chilling novel of a Polish Jewish girl and 20 American Jewish men con-
demned to die in a concentration camp.

Lustig, Arnost. Darkness Casts No Shadow. N.Y.: Avon Books, 1977.

    Novel about escape from a Nazi death train.

Lustig, Arnost. Night and Hope. N.Y.: Avon Books, 1978.

    Seven stories which relate what it was like to grow up in the Nazi camp of
Terezin.

Malamud, Bernard. The Fixer. N.Y.: Dell Publishing Co., 1974.

    A novel based on the Mendel Beillis case about an alleged ritual murder in
Russia.

Mannes, Marya. "Dad, What's a Conscience?" Newsweek, 15 April 1974.

    A discussion of the loss of conscience in modern life.

Manvell, Roger. S.S. and Gestapo. N.Y.: Ballantine, 1969.

    A pictorial account of the growth of the S.S. and Gestapo, and their
activities in the death camps and in the East.

May, Rollo. Man's Search for Himself. N.Y.: W. W. Norton, 1953.

    An excellent book about the uncertainty and anxiety of modern people, and
the need for courage and real awareness of self.

May, Rollo. Power and Innocence. N.Y.: Dell Publishing Co., 1972.

    An explanation of the modern origins of violence.

McCarthy, Edward V., Jr. The Pied Piper of Helfenstein. N.Y.: Doubleday,
1975.

    The mystery of World War II Scarlet Pimpernel who rescued hundreds of
children from Nazi concentration camps.

McCuen, Gary. The Racist Reader. Minneapolis: Greenhaven Press, 1974.

    A collection of readings and cartoons which sharply demonstrate the nature
of racism.

Meggysey, Dave. "Out of Their League." Berkeley: Ramparts. 1970, pp. 46-8, 144-7.

An excellent personal account of a young man's total experience playing football.

Mermelstein, Mel. By Bread Alone. Los Angeles: Crescent Publications, 1979.

A survivor's account of his experience in a series of concentration camps. Includes photographs and newspaper accounts.

Merrick, Tony. The American Woman: Her Image and Her Roles. Middletown, Conn.: Xerox, 1975.

A collection of readings about American women which includes several studies of the "Motive to Avoid Success."

Meltzer, Milton. World of Our Father: The Jews of Eastern Europe. N.Y.: Farrar, Straus and Giroux, 1974. Dell, 1976. Paper.

A picture of Jewish life in Eastern Europe using eye-witness accounts.

Miale, Florence, and Michael Selzer. The Nuremberg Mind. N.Y.: Quadrangle, 1975.

A psychological study of Nazi leaders based on interviews of prisoners awaiting trial at Nuremberg.

Milgram, Stanley. Obedience to Authority. N.Y.: Harper and Row, 1975.

A discussion by the creator of the famous and controversial "shock" experiment which began as a study of the German tendency to obey.

Mitford, Jessica. Kind and Usual Punishment. N.Y.: Vintage Books, 1973.

A discussion of the failure of the American prison system, including evidence of the use of prisoners as guinea pigs for medical and drug experiments.

Moffett, James and Kenneth McElheny, eds. Points of View: An Anthology of Short Stories. N.Y.: New American Library, 1966.

A compilation of short stories by some of the world's greatest writers.

Montagu, Ashley. On Being Human. N.Y.: Hawthorne Books, 1966.

A well-written critique of those who believe that humans are basically war-like and competitive.

Morris, Desmond. The Naked Ape. N.Y.: Dell Publishing Co., 1967.

A former British zookeeper draws a direct tie between animal and human behavior.

Morse, Arthur D. While Six Million Died: A Chronicle of American Apathy.
    N.Y.: Random House, 1968. Hart, 1975.

    A disturbing account of the U.S. inability to mount an effort to save
    European Jews.

Moskin, Marietta. I am Rosemarie. N.Y.: Day, 1972.

    An author of juvenile books, now living in America fictionalizes her expe-
    riences as a child sent from her home in Holland to a concentration camp.

Mosse, George L. The Crisis of German Ideology: Intelligence Origins of the
    Third Reich. N.Y.: Grosset and Dunlap, 1964.

    A scholarly study by the well-known European historian which deals with the
    origins of Nazi thinking.

Mosse, George L. Germans and Jews: The Right, the Left, and the Search for a
    'Third Force" in Pre-Nazi Germany. N.Y.: Howard Fertig, 1970.

    A collection of essays which explores German totalitarianism and its
    relation to anti-Semitism.

Mosse, George. L., ed. Nazi Culture: Intellectual, Cultural and Social Life in
    the Third Reich. N.Y.: Grosset & Dunlap, 1966. Paper.

    An anthology detailing the cultural and social aspects of Nazism.

Muller, Filip. Eyewitness Auschwitz. N.Y.: Stein and Day, 1979.

    The author's experience as a member of the Sonderkommando at Auschwitz.

Myrer, Anton. "The Giant in the Tube." Harpers, November 1972, pp. 40-56.

    An able discussion of why football has superseded baseball as the most
    popular sport in America.

"The Nazi Hunt: One Case." Philadelphia Inquirer. 24 October 1976.

    A brief discussion of the case against alleged war criminal Valerian Trifa.

Neilands, J.B., et al. Harvet of Death. N.Y.: Free Press, 1972.

    A scientific account of the use of chemical warfare in Vietnam, and its
    danger to both user and victim.

Neshamit, Sarah. The Children of Mapu Street. N.Y.: Jewish Publication
    Society, 1970.

    A heart-breaking fictional account of the various fates of each of a group
    of neighborhood Jewish children in Kovno, Lithuania, from the time of Nazi
    occupation until the end of World War II.

Neuerbourg, Nans. "Holocaust Stirs Memories of Switzerland's Epoch of Guilt."
    Atlantic City Press. 13 May 1979, p. 12.

    An article which throws new light on the official policy of the Swiss
    government during World War II.

Nichlas, Marta. Bangladesh: The Birth of a Nation. Interculture, 1973.

    A thorough discussion of the origin of this nation.

Nolte, Ernest. Three Faces of Fascism. N.Y.: New American Library, 1965.
    Frederick Fell, 1960. Crest, 1973. Paper.

    An eyewitness account by a Jewish doctor who volunteered to become a tool
    of the S.S. in order to stay alive. Includes discussion of S.S. medical
    doctors, including Dr. Mengele.

O'Brien, Tim. If I Die in a Combat Zone. N.Y.: Delacorte Press, 1973.

    A well-written war novel describing the experiences of an army unit.

Okpaku, Joseph. Nigeria, Dilemma of Nationhood: An Analysis of the Biafran
    Conflict. Connecticut: Greenwhich Press, 1974.

    A valuable surce for information about the civil war in Nigeria.

Orgel, Doris. A Certain Magic. N.Y.: Dial, 1976.

    A novel about an eleven year old searching the past for clues and details
    about her aunt who had escaped from the Nazis during World War II.

Orwell, George. 1984. N.Y.: American Library, 1971. Paper.

    A compelling novel about a negative Utopia and totalitarianism control.

Strom, Margot Stern and William S. Parsons. Facing History and Ourselves:
    Holocaust and Human Behavior. Watertown, MA: International Educations,
    1982.

    A full curriculum including readings and activities.

Payne, Robert. The Life and Death of Adolf Hitler. N.Y.: Praeger Publishers,
    1973.

    A basic biography of the dictator's life, includes interesting details.

Peck, Richard, ed. Sounds and Silences. N.Y.: Dell, 1972.

    A good collection of poetry and songs which includes selections by W.H.
    Auden, the Beatles, and many others about loneliness, illusion, dissent,
    and war.

Petry, Ann. Harriet Tubman: Conductor of the Underground Railway.
        :Archway, 1971. Paper.

    A biography of the famous anti-slavery leader who helped smuggle slaves out
    of the South.

Phillips, Peter. The Tragedy of Nazi Germany. N.Y.: Praeger Publishers,
    1969.

    An account of the German acceptance of Nazi ideas and philosophy, and its
    effect on the people. Chapter One is excellent.

Poor, Harold L. Kurt Tucholsky and the Ordeal of Germany 1914-1935. N.Y.:
    Charles Scribner's Sons, 1968.

    A discussion of the famous Jewish social critic of Weimar, Gemany.

Postman, Neil. Crazy Talk, Stupid Talk. N.Y.: Delacourt Press, 1976.

    A discussion of language and how it can mask real motives and interests.

"The Pull of the Sun Moon." The New York Times Magazine, 30 April 1976.

    A discussion of the appeal of the largest religious cult in America, the
    "Moonies."

Raab, Ear. The Anatomy of Nazism. N.Y.: ADL, 1961.

    A brief account of the background, philosophy and components of Nazism.

Rabinowitz, Dorothy. New Lives: Survivors of the Holocaust Living in America.
    N.Y.: Alfred A. Knopf, 1976.

    A study of the lives of Holocaust survivors living in America.

Rabinsky, Leatrice and Beatrice Mann. Journal of Conscience. Distributed by
    ADL.

    American high school students visit the camps.

"Rats Without Room," Population Control, Education Publications (Xerox), 1971.

    An excellent review of the Calhoun rat experiment dealing with the effects
    of population on human behavior.

Reich, Wilhelm. The Mass Psychology of Fascism. N.Y.: Farrar, Straus, and
    Giroux, 1970.

    Describes fascism as the expression of the irrational character structure
    of humans whose primary biolgical needs and impulses have been suppressed
    for many years.

Reid, Robert H. "Pope John Paul at Auschwitz," Philadelphia Inquirer, 8 June
    1979, pp. 11A-12A.

    The Pope's visit in 1979.

Reitlinger, Gerald. The S.S.: Alibi of a Nation 1922-1945. N.Y.: Viking
Press, 1968.

A classic book by the German historian about the origin and function of the
S.S. during the war.

Remarque, Erich Maria. All Quiet on the Western Front. N.Y.: Fawcett, 1961.

The classic German anti-war novel of the twenties that was banned by the
Nazis.

Rhodes, Anthony. Propaganda: The Art of Persuasion: World War II. N.Y.:
Chelsea House Publishers, 1980.

An excellent visual compendium of all forms of propaganda used by the
Allied and Axis powers in the World War II period.

Richter, Hans Peter. Friedrich. N.Y.: Dell, 1973.

An excellent juvenile novel about the friendship between a German and a
Jewish boy in Hitler's Germany.

Richter, Hans Peter. I Was There. N.Y.: Holt, Rinehart & Winston, 1972.

A fine account of the Hitler Youth Movement in Germany as told by an eye-
witness.

Ringelblum, Emmanuel. Notes from the Warsaw Ghetto. N.Y.: McGraw-Hill, 1958.

An eyewitness account of the day-to-day life in the Warsaw Ghetto by an
historian.

Rousseau, Jean Jacques. Discourse on the Origins of Inequality. N.Y.: Simon
and Schuster, 1964.

A view of society as the "devil" which produces the "evil in humans.

Rubenstein, Richard L. The Cunning of History: Mass Death and the American
Future. N.Y.: Harper & Row, 1975.

A discussion of the effect of bureaucracy, technology, and the notion of
"superfluous people" on wholesale extermination.

Rubin, Arnold P. The Evil That Men Do. N.Y.: Julian Messner, 1977, Bantam,
1979.

A well-written overview of the Holocaust.

Samuel, Maurice. Blood Accusation. N.Y.: Alfred A. Knopf, 1966.

A narrative about one of the most famous "blood ritual" trials occurring in
Czarist Russia.

Samuels, Gertrude. Mottele. N.Y.: Signet Boks, 1976.

A fictionalized account of a child's survival in the forest of Eastern
Europe.

Satyaprakash, ed. Bangladesh: A Select Bibliography.   : South Asia Books,
    1977.

An exhaustive bibliography with ample listings on the mass murders.

Schoenberner, Gerhard. The Yellow Star: The Persecution of the Jews in
    Europe, 1933-1945. N.Y.: Bantam, 1973. Paper.

A pictorial history of the persecution of the Jews in Europe, 1933-45.

Scholl, Inge. Students Against Tyranny: The Resistance of the White Rose,
    Munich, 1942-1943.

Recalls the efforts of the famous White Rose resistance movement in Munich.

Schulman, Charles. What It Means To Be a Jew. N.Y.: Crown, 1960.

Discusses the character, ethical foundation, and philososphy of Judaism.

Schwarz-Bart, Andre. Last of the Just. Trans. by Stephen Becker from the
    French. N.Y.: Atheneum, 1960. Paper, 1977. Bantam, Paper.

Fictional narrative about Ernie Levy, last of a hereditary line of 36
righteous men for whose sake God allows the world to continue.

Sereny, Gitta. Into that Darkness. N.Y.: McGraw-Hill, 1974.

Interviews and psychological analyses of Franz Stangl, the commandant of
Treblinka, and other Nasis: the Nazi "Euthanasia Program," and death camps.
Excellent.

Sefton, Delmer. Weimar Germany. N.Y.: American Heritage Press.

An overview of the struggle during the Weimer period. Includes striking
paintings and cartoons.

Shearer, Cody. "Anniversary for a Long Unsung Hero," Philadelphia Inquirer,
    22 August 1979.

The story of one man's personal sacrifice during the Civil Rights Movement
of the 1960's.

Shirer, William L. The Rise and Fall of the Third Reich: A History of Nazi
    Germany. N.Y.: Simon and Schuster, 1960. Paper in 2 vols; also Fawcett
    World, 1972. Paper.

A classic work.

Singer, Isaac Bashevis. The Spinoza of Market Street. N.Y.: Avon, 1970.

A collection of some of the Nobel Prize winner's most intriguing short
stories.

"Skinner's Utopia: Panacea, or Path to Hell?" Time. 2 September 1971, pp.
    47-53.

An overview of the career and views of the famous behaviorist.

"Slaughter of the Innocents," <u>Newsweek</u>,, 2 July 1973.

   Tells the story of the murder of the Bahutu tribe in the African state of
   Barundi.

Snell, Bradford. "G.M. and the Nazis," <u>Ramparts</u>, 1974, pp. 14-16.

   An article which relates American corporate involvement and the rise of
   Nazi Germany.

Snyder, Louis. <u>The Encyclopedia of the Third Reich</u>. N.Y.: McGraw-Hill, 1976.

   A handy reference.

Social Science Staff of the Educational Research Council of America.
   <u>Prejudice and Discrimination</u>. Boston: Allyn and Bacon, Inc., 1973.

   A good explanation of the origins and motives behind prejudice and discrimination. Effective methods of dealing with prejudice are offered.

Solzhenitsyn, Alexander. <u>The Gulag Archipelago 1918-1956: An Experiment in
   Literary Investigation</u>. N.Y.: Harper & Row; Parts I & II, 1974. Parts III
   & IV, 1976. Paper.

   A first-hand account of a political prisoner's life in a brutal Soviet
   prison camp by the Nobel laureate.

Sommerfelt, Aimee. <u>Miriam</u>. N.Y.: Scholastic, 1972.

   Juvenile literature about the survival of a teenager in Nazi-occupied
   Norway.

Speer, Albert. <u>Inside the Third Reich</u>. N.Y.: Avon Books, 1970.

   An inside look at Hitler and his Reich by ex-Nazi Minister Speer. Written
   after his release from Spandau prison.

Stadtler, Bea. <u>The Holocaust: A History of Courage and Resistance</u>. N.Y.:
   ADL/Behrman House, 1974. Also paper.

   A simplified history of the Holocaust emphasizing resistance.

Stein, George. <u>Hitler: Great Lives Observed</u>. Englewood Cliffs: Prentice-
   Hall, 1968.

   A portrait of the career and personality of Adolf Hitler.

Steinbeck, John. <u>The Grapes of Wrath</u>. N.Y.: Viking Press, 1939.

   The famous Depression novel which describes the trials of the Joad family
   of Oklahoma in the California labor camps.

Steiner, Jean-Francois. <u>Trablinka</u>. Translated from the French by Helen
   Weaver. N.Y.: Simon & Schuster, 1967. Signet. Paper.

   A documentary novel about the Treblinka extermination camp. Intended to
   dispel the notion that all victims marched unresisting to their deaths.

Steinetz, Lucy Y. and David M. Szonyi, eds. <u>Living After the Holocaust:
    Reflections by the Post-War Generation</u>. N.Y.: Bloch, 1976. Paper.

    Essays, poetry, and interviews showing how children of Holocaust survivors
    attempt to deal with their parents' special problems.

Storr, Anthony. <u>Human Aggression</u>. N.Y.: Bantam Books, 1968.

    A discussion of the role of aggression and hostility in human life.

Suhl, Yuri, editor and translator. <u>They Fought Back: The Story of the Jewish
    Resistance in Nazi Europe</u>. N.Y.: Schocken Books, 1975. (ADL) Paper.

    A collection of true stories and documents which tell of organizers and
    heroes of the Jewish underground, ghettos, and camps.

Suhl, Yuri. <u>Uncle Misha's Partisans</u>. N.Y.: Four Winds Press (Scholastic),
    1973.

    A twelve year old escapes to the woods and joins a famous resistance
    fighter. Fiction.

Switzer, Ellen. <u>How Democracy Failed</u>. N.Y.: Atheneum, 1975.

    Interviews of Germans who recall the impact of Nazism on their lives as
    teenagers.

Szajkowski, Zosa. <u>An Illustrated Sourcebook on the Holocaust</u>. Vols. I, II,
    III. N.Y.: Ktav, 1977.

    An excellent collection of public materials designed by the Nazi propaganda
    machine and its non-German collaborators to induce greater anti-Semitism.

Tanner, Ogden. <u>Stress</u>. N.Y.: Time-Life Books, 1976.

    Includes discussion of the French people's response to German occupation
    during World War II.

Taylor, Telford. <u>Nuremberg and Vietnam</u>. N.Y.: Times Books, 1972.

    A discussion of the similarities between the war crimes of Germany and
    those of the U.S. Written by a U.S. prosecutor at the Nuremberg trials.

Terlouw, Jan. <u>Winter in Wartime</u>. N.Y.: McGraw-Hill, 1976.

    A novel about a young boy in Holland who joins the resistance.

Thalmann, Rita. <u>Crystal Night</u>. N.Y.: Holocaust Library, 1980. (ADL)

    A historical account of the events surrounding the rioting which led to
    terrorization of Jews throughout Germany on the night of November 9-10,
    1938.

Thomas, Gordon and Max Morgan Witts. <u>Voyage of the Damned</u>. N.Y.: Stein and
     Day, 1974.

     An account of the voyage of the St. Louis as it carried its Jewish passen-
     gers back to certain death.

Rabinsky, Lea. <u>Times of the Holocaust: No Excuse for Apathy</u>. Cleveland
     Heights, Ohio: Cleveland Heights School.

     A good compilation of various materials with which to study the Holocaust.

Timerman, Jacobo. <u>Prisoner Without a Name. Cell Without a Number</u>. N.Y.:
     Knoff, 1980.

     A newspaperman's account of his imprisonment and torture in Argentina.

Toland, John. <u>Adolf Hitler</u>. N.Y.: Doubleday, 1976.

     A massive study of Hitler which draws on interviews of people connected
     with the Fuhrer.

Toll, Nelly. <u>Without Surrender: Art of the Holocaust</u>. Philadelphia:
     Running Press, 1978.

     Tells the story of the camps through the drawings of inmates, including the
     author's.

Torgerson, Dial. "Assault of Holocaust," <u>Philadelphia Inquirer</u>, 9 November
     1980, p. 1H.

     A news article which explores the new interpretations of the Holocaust
     which deny the murder of six million Jews.

Toynbee, Arnold. <u>Armenian Atrocities</u>. N.Y.: Tankian Publishing, 1975.

     The famous historian's narrative of the genesis and execution of genocide
     against the Armenians.

Trumbo, Dalton. <u>Johnny Got His Gun</u>. N.Y.: Bantam Books, 1972.

     A devastating nvella about the senseless destruction of human life in
     Veitnam seen through the eyes of one man.

Trunk, Isaiah. <u>Judenrat</u>. N.Y.: Stein and Day, 1977.

     A major study of the role of Jewish communal leaders in the ghetto.

Turnbull, Colin. "The Mountain People," <u>Intellectual Digest</u>, April 1973,
     pp. 49-56.

     The noted anthropologists'account of an African people who have lost the
     capacity for love.

Uris, Leon. _Mila 18_. N.Y.: Doubleday, 1961. Bantam. Paper.

    A novel about a street in the Warsaw Ghetto where the Jews made their last
    stand.

Uris, Leon. _BQ VII_. N.Y.: Doubleday, 1972. Bantam. Paper.

    A suspenseful novel about a court trial involving a N.Y. writer and the
    doctor he claims participated in concentration camp experiments.

Vietnam Veterans Against the War. _The Winter Soldier Investigation_. Boston:
    Beacon Press, 1972.

    Testimonay offered by anti-Veitnam veterans about their training and their
    beliefs regarding the real motives for the war.

Volavkova, H., ed. _I Never Saw Another Butterfly_. N.Y.: McGraw-Hill, 1964.

    Drawings and poetry by children in the Terezin concentration camp.

Von Blum, Paul. _The Art of Social Conscience_. N.Y.: Universe Books, 1976.

    An overview of the social responsibility of the artist, including chapters
    on both German expressionism and Holocaust.

Wainwright, Loudon. "The Dying Girl That No One Helped," _Life_. 10 April 1964.

    The spectators' view of what happened to Kitty Genovese.

Waite, Robert G.L. _The Psychopathic God_. N.Y.: New American Library, 1977.

    A psychological study of Adolf Hitler. Builds on the earlier work of
    William Langer.

Walzer, Michael. "The Moral Problem of Refugees." _New Republic_ issue, pp.
    15-17.

    An interesting ethical discussion of America's struggle over responsibility
    for refugees.

Weisberg, Alex. _Desperate Mission_. N.Y.: Criterion Books, 1958.

    An account of the Joel Brand mission to save Hungarian Jews in 1944.
    Brand, a leader of the Hungarian Jewish underground, was offered a deal of
    "blood for trucks "by Adolf Eichmann.

Weiss, Peter. _The Investigation_. N.Y.: Pocket Books, 1966.

    This play recreates the testimony in the Auschwitz Trial. Very well done,
    although lacking in action.

Weiss, Peter. _Marat/Sade_. N.Y.: Pocket Books, 1971.

    A magnificent play about much more than mental patients in a French asylum
    at the time of Napoleon. The play is a confrontation between the ideas of
    the revolutionary Jean Paul Marat and the controvesial Marquis de Sade.

Weglyn, Michi. <u>Years of Infamy</u>. N.Y.: William Morrow and Company, 1976.

Discusses the internment of Japanese-Americans during World War II in "re-
location centers."

Werfel, Franz. <u>Forty Days of Musa Dagh</u>. N.Y.: Viking, 1934.

The classic literary account of the heroic attempt by Armenians to hold out
against the Turks.

"Why You Do What You Do: Sociobiology: A New Theory of Behavior." <u>Time</u>.
1 August 1977, pp. 54-67.

A difficult but rewarding discussion of the basic beliefs of the neo-
Darwinist school of thought.

Wiesel, Elie. <u>The Accident</u>. N.Y.: Avon Books, 1974.

The author, a survivor of the Nazi horror, weaves his experiences into the
story of a young man who was obsessed by the horrors of the camp and eventually loses his will to live.

Wiesel, Elie. <u>Dawn</u>. N.Y.: Avon Books, 1970.

A tense novel about a young Jew faced with the duty of executing a British
hostage in occupied Palestine.

Wiesel, Elie. <u>The Gates of the Forest</u>. N.Y.: Avon Books, 1966.

Surviving the Holocaust at the cost of innocence, a young man struggles to
exorcise the guilt of a generation that produced Hitler.

Wiesel, Elie. "Lost and Found Again." <u>Commonweal</u>, July 1974.

Discusses faith in God in the death camps.

Wiesel, Elie. <u>Messengers of God</u>. N.Y.: Pocket Books, 1977.

A brilliant reinterpretation of the stories of Adam and Eve, Cain and Abel,
Job, and other Biblical figures.

Wiesel, Elie. "Biafra, The End," "Accomplices." <u>A Jew Today</u>.

Suggests that in at least two contemporary examples of genocide, the world
has chosen to do nothing.

Wiesel, Elie. <u>Night</u>. N.Y.: Hill and Wang. Avon Books, 1972.

The author's personal account of his years in concentration camps, and the
loss of his family. Also deals with his moral dilemma regarding religious
faith and conviction.

Wiesel, Elie. <u>One Generation After</u>. N.Y.: Avon, 1971. Paper.

Essays and stories deal with one generation after the Holocaust.

Wiesel, Elie. <u>The Town Beyond the Wall</u>. N.Y.: Avon Books, 1967.

 The novel of a concentration camp survivor who returns to his home in Communist Hungary only to be imprisoned again.

Williams, Edgard. "40 Days of Musa Dagh." <u>Philadelphia Inquirer</u>, 19 September 1980, pp. 1-2B.

 A news article about an Armenian couple who survived the genocide earlier this century.

Williams, Roger M. "Why Wasn't Auschwitz Bombed?" <u>Commentary</u>, March, 1978.

 Describes as "an American moral tragedy" the reasons for failure to bomb the death camp.

Wills, Garry. "Holocaust Was Hard to Believe." <u>Philadelphia Inquirer</u>, 6 August 1980.

 An editorial asking why humans have so much difficulty believeing the occurrence of atrocities.

Wisenthal, Simon. <u>The Sunflower</u>. N.Y.: Schocken Books, 1976.

 Challenges the reader to feel the anguish of a young Jew who is asked for forgiveness by a dying Nazi.

Woodward C. Vann. <u>Tom Watson: Agrarian Rebel</u>. N.Y.: Oxford Press, 1963.

 A biography which includes a description of the Leo Frank case which raised the specter of anti-Semitism and "blood ritual" in early twentieth century America.

Woodward, Kenneth and Eloise Salholz. "Sisters of the Third World." <u>Newsweek</u>, 22 December 1980, p. 75.

 Deals with the murder of three Mary Knoll sisters in El Salvador, and explains the special nature of the Mary Knoll philosophy.

Wyman, David. "Why Auschwitz Was Never Bombed." <u>Commentary</u>, May 1978, pp. 37-46.

 An explosive interpretation of why the Allies were unwilling to bomb Auschwitz.

Yinger, J. Milton. <u>Anti-Semitism: A Case Study in Prejudice and Discrimination</u>. N.Y.: ADL, 1964.

 A learned account of the impact of prejudice and anti-Semitism.

Act of Faith
28 minutes/black and white/not cleared for TV/also 3/4" video/ADL
    A first-hand account of how the Danes saved their Jewish countrymen from
    Nazi extermination. Filmed in Denmark.

After the First
14 minutes/color/Franciscan Communications
    In this dramatization of a 12-year-old boy being taken on his first hunting
    trip by his father, the boy enjoys learning to use a gun on inanimate
    objects. His feelings change when the targets of their shooting become
    rabbits.

All Quiet on the Western Front
105 minutes/black and white/Universal 16
    Based on the anti-war novel by Erich Maria Remarque, the first version was
    made in Germany in the late 1920's and was later banned. A recent TV
    version with Richard Thomas and Ernest Borgnine was done well.

Ambulance
15 minutes/black and white/Alden
    A group of children together with their teacher are slowly herded into an
    isolated area. They are loaded into an ambulance, where they are entrapped
    and gassed. For upper level high school.

The Anatomy of Nazism
filmstrip/55 frames/color/ADL
    An historic presentation of social, cultural, economic and political
    workings of fascism in Hitler Germany.
    Special class kit: 1 filmstrip, "The Anatomy of Nazism." 30 copies of "The
    Anatomy of Nazism" booklet. 6 copies of "The Third Reich in Perspective."
    Special teacher kit: 1 filmstrip, "The Anatomy of Nazism." 1 copy of "The
    Anatomy of Nazism" study booklet. 1 copy of "The Third Reich in
    Perspective" resource unit.

Andersonville
video/color/PBS
    TV production of the famous post-Civil War trial about a Southern prison
    camp.

The Armenian Case
43 minutes/color/Atlantis
    Accounts by survivors of Turkish atrocities. European and American
    eyewitnesses recall the chilling historical events. "The Forgotten
    Genocide," abridged version.

Avenue of the Just
55 minutes/color/ADL/also 3/4" video
    Dramatically documents the role played by non-Jews in the rescue of Jews.

Black History: Lost, Stolen or Strayed
54 minutes/color/ADL
    This classic film narrated by Bill Cosby describes how Blacks have been
    depicted in American culture and speculates about the future direction of
    Black Americans.

The Blue Angel
112 minutes/black and white/Janus or Museum of Modern Art
    A German film of the 1920's about an old professor who falls in love with a
    dance hall singer.

Cabaret
123 minutes/color/Cinema Guild
    A feature film, originally a Bob Fosse play, about social life in Weimar
    Germany. Some powerful scenes show the slow rise of the Nazis. Based on
    The Berlin Stories by Christopher Isherwood.

The Cabinet of Dr. Caligari
50 minutes/black and white/Films, Inc. or Museum of Modern Art
    An important German film of the early 1920's about a crazed scientist who
    could manipulate others to murder. A vision of the future.

Changing of the System
filmstrip/96 frames/sound/Social Studies School Service
    Explores some of the alternatives available to produce social change in
    contemporary America.

Corrida Interdite
10 minutes/color/Pyramid
    A film showing a series of bullfights, leading the viewer to ask "Why?"

Cruel Diagonals
11 minutes/black and white/Films, Inc.
    An Eastern European war story about a young boy's introduction to death and
    conflict.

Day in the Life of Jonathan Mole
33 minutes/black and white/ADL
    A Canadian film about a bitter and prejudiced man who one night dreams he
    has the power and authority to judge the "lesser" minorities.

Dead Birds
83 minutes/color/CRM-McGraw Hill
    An interesting anthropological study of two tribes in New Guinea constantly
    warring against each other.

Death of a Peasant
10 minutes/color/Mass Media Associates
    A film about one man's decision to die on his own terms.

The Death of Socrates
45 minutes/black and white/Time-Life/(BBC)
27 minutes/black and white/CRM-McGraw Hill
    Films about the philosopher's decision to die.

Deciding Right from Wrong: The Dilemma of Morality Today
160 frames/color/script/record or cassette/Center for Humanities
     Focuses on the judgment-making process in a world that often insists that
     there are no moral judgments to be made.

Decision to Drop the Bomb: Hiroshima and Nagasaki
35 minutes/black and white/Films, Inc.
     A film which explores the crucial choice to use the first atomic bomb.

The Deer Hunter
color/Swank
     A feature film starring Robert DeNiro about the experience of several
     Americans in Vietnam and the effects of the war upon them.

Denmark '43
22 minutes/color/Jewish Media Center
     A present-day Danish high school teacher guides his students through a re-
     enactment on location of the courageous rescue of Jews by Danish fishing
     villagers during the Nazi occupation.

Diary of Anne Frank
170 minutes/black and white/Films, Inc.
     Millie Perkins, Joseph Schildkraut, Shelly Winters. Directed by George
     Stevens.

The Distorted Image: Stereotype and Caricature in American Popular Graphics
1850-1922
60 slides/or 28 minute filmstrip/color/Discussion Guide
     Cartoons and illustrations which reveal the extent and nature of
     stereotyping affecting all minority groups in the U.S.

Enemy of the People
20 minutes/color/Time-Life
     A film first shown on "60 Minutes" about a man who risks his own future by
     criticizing the quality of Lockheed aircraft. Thought provoking.

Exodus
207 minutes/color/United Artists
     A feature film depicting the smuggling of Holocaust survivors into Palestine
     before it became Israel.

Fence at Minidaka
30 minutes/color/KOMO-TV, Seattle
     The World War II Japanese relocation camp at Minidaka, Idaho, is visited by
     a Sansei television reporter.

The Fifth Horseman Is Fear
100 minutes/black and white/available in subtitled and dubbed versions/Films,
Inc.
     A Czech feature film depicting the Nazi takeover of Prague.

The Fixer
132 minutes/color/Films, Inc.
    A feature film about a young Russian Jew who is unjustly accused of "ritual
    murder." Based on a real case in the early 20th century and the book by
    Arthur Miller.

Free Will and Utopias
filmstrips
    An excellent discussion of the B.F. Skinner theory of man versus the theory
    of those who favor free will. Forces students to think about why they act.

From Kaiser to Fuehrer
26 minutes/black and white/CRM-McGraw Hill (CBS-TV "20th Century" Series)
    The story of the ill-fated Weimar Republic, set up by forward-looking
    Germans after World War I, and sent to its death in 1933 by a combination of
    depression, inexperience of the Germans at democracy, and the doubts of many
    of its adherents.

Galileo: The Challenge of Reason
28 minutes/color/Learning Corporation of America
    A film about the famous scientist's confrontation with the church.

Games of Angels
13 minutes/color/Pyramid
    A Polish interpretation of the concentration camps.

The Garden of the Finzi-Continis
103 minutes/color/Cinema Five
    The decline and fall of Italian Jewry seen through the life of one family.
    Feature film.

Genocide
52 minutes/color/ADL
    The history of the "Final Solution" from the 1920's to 1945. Narrated by
    Sir Lawrence Olivier, this is part of the British produced "World at War"
    television series. Excellent overview.

Gestapo: A Learning Experience about the Holocaust: A Simulation
Social Studies School Service
    The simulation board game challenges students to survive in Hitler's Germany
    while maintaining values identified in the game as important.

Guilt by Reason of Race
51 minutes/color/Indiana University Film Library or NBC Educational Enterprises
    A 1972 television documentary which features many members of the Japanese
    American community.

Hangman
12 minutes/color/CRM-McGraw Hill
    An allegorical poem in which the coward in the film, who has let others die
    to protect himself, becomes the hangman's final victim. Animated film based
    on moral responsibility in today's world.

The Hand
19 minutes/color/CRM-McGraw Hill
    Creative and thought-provoking animated film by Jiri Trinka about the
    effects of totalitarianism on one innocent puppet.

Harold and Maude
91 minutes/color/Films, Inc.
    An inspiring motion picture about an old woman who gives life to a young
    boy. Ruth Gordon and Bud Cort star.

Hiroshima/Nagasaki
16 minutes/black and white/Center for Mass Communications
    Footage of the two Japanese cities after the atomic bombs were dropped in
    1945.

Hitler
26 minutes/color/Learning Corporation of America
    A "fictional" interview with Hitler in which he expresses his philosophy.

Hitler and the Germans
filmstrips/color/cassette or record/Listening Library
    Presents a panorama of Germany from 1933 to 1938 when Hitler felt strong
    enough at home to embark on a world takeover. Visuals from Nazi archives.

Hitler's Executioners
78 minutes/black and white/Films, Inc.
    Utilizing official war records and newsreel clips, this documentary gives an
    on-the-spot picture report of the rise and fall of Hitler's Third Reich,
    including his rise to power, promises, the Nazi war machine, and finally the
    Nuremberg Trials.

Holocaust
4 films/also video cassettes/Learning Corporation of America
    The NBC television drama by Gerald Green that can be severely criticized yet
    it is of some value in introducing aspects of the Holocaust to the general
    public.
    Part I -- The Gathering Storm / 144 minutes
    Part II -- The Road to Babi Yar / 99 minutes
    Part III -- The Final Solution / 94 minutes
    Part IV -- The Saving Remnant / 102 minutes

The Holocaust
filmstrips/color/record or cassette/Audio-Visual Narrative Arts
    Part one describes the spirit and suffering of the Jews in ghettos and death
    camps. Part two traces the long history of European anti-Semitism that
    paved the way for the Nazi destruction of the Jewish population. Told in
    the words of those who walked through this "geography of hell."

The Holocaust: 1933-45
20 posters (23" x 29")/Viewer's Guide and Suggestions for Display/ADL
    A series of black and white posters beginning with pre-Holocaust Jewish life
    in Europe and going on to depict the growth of Nazism and anti-Semitism, the
    ghettos, death camps, liberation, the Nuremberg Trials and the building of
    new lives in Israel.

An Inquiry into the Nature of Man: His Inhumanity and His Humanity
slides/sound/Teacher's Guide/Center for the Humanities
     Are human beings basically good or evil? Part one examines our inhumanity
     to each other, confronting students with the question of whether inhumanity
     is part of our very nature. Part two investigates the essence of our
     humanity toward one another - our sometimes fierce struggle to express that
     which is best about ourselves.

Joseph Schultz
14 minutes/color/ADL
     Vital questions concerning personal moral choice versus obedience to
     authority are raised in this film. Based on an actual incident, Schultz
     refuses to execute a group of villagers and joins them at the wall. He was
     executed.

Judgment at Mineola
14 minutes/color/ADL
     An accused war criminal, Boleslav Maikevskis, living on Long Island, faces
     deportation. Mike Wallace and a CBS "60 Minutes" crew interview some
     Mineola residents regarding their opinions.

Judgment at Nuremberg
186 minutes/black and white/United Artists/also filmstrip/ADL
     Nazis on trial judged by international tribune. Feature film with Spencer
     Tracy as the American judge; Maximillian Schell, the defense attorney;
     Montgomery Clift and Judy Garland, two of the victims who gave testimony.
     Directed by Stanley Kramer.

The Juggler
80 minutes/black and white/Films, Inc.
     A refugee, once a juggler on the European stage, finds a new home in Israel
     but cannot overcome his obsessive fear of the police instilled by the
     Nazis. Feature film.

Julia
117 minutes/color/Films, Inc.
     Feature film with Jane Fonda and Vanessa Redgrave which focuses on
     experiences during 1938-1945. Based on Lillian Hellman's autobiography.

Lament of the Reservation
24 minutes/color/CRM-McGraw Hill
     A film narrated by Marlon Brando showing the life of those American Indians
     who have chosen to remain on reservations. A very moving conclusion.

The Last Nazi
71 minutes/color/black and white/Learning Corporation of America
     Several years after his release from Spandau Prison where he completed his
     20-year sentence for war crimes, Albert Speer is interviewed by Canadian
     reporter Patrick Watson.

The Last Rabbi
30 minutes/black and white/National Academy for Adult Jewish Studies
     This film portrays the heroism and courage of the victims of the Warsaw
     Ghetto.

Lies My Father Told Me
102 minutes/color/subtitles/Films, Inc.
    Interesting Canadian film by Jan Kadar about the conflict between
    generations.

The Life That Disappeared
80 slides/16-minute tape cassette/16-page guide/black and white/rental: Jewish
Media Service/purchase: Scholastic
    This slide/tape program, photographed and narrated by Roman Vishniac,
    provides an intimate glimpse of everyday Jewish life in Poland's cities and
    villages in the years immediately preceding the Holocaust.

Lord of the Flies
black and white/Clem Williams
    Disturbing feature film about a group of English school boys shipwrecked on
    a tropical island. Based on the novel by William Golding.

The Lottery
18 minutes/color/Encyclopaedia Britannica
    Based on the Shirley Jackson story, the film is about a small American town
    holding a lottery which turns out to be a ritual for selecting someone who
    is to be stoned to death.

M
99 minutes/black and white/Films, Inc.
    A 1920's German film with Peter Lorre about a man who could not help himself
    from committing murder.

The Magician
13 minutes/black and white/Mass Media Ministries
    In this Polish-made allegory, a group of young boys walking the beach are
    attracted to a carnival shooting gallery. A military officer in the guise
    of a magician entices them to use the rifles, trains them to shoot dolls,
    drills them in marching, and finally marches them off to war.

The Making of the German Nation: 1815-1945
4 filmstrips/color/2 records or cassettes/manual or automatic/Teacher's
Notes/Educational Audio-Visual
    Part I deals with German history from 1815 to 1871.
    Part II from 1871 to 1918.
    Part III from 1918 to 1933.
    Part IV from 1933 to 1945.

Man Against Man: A Study in Aggression and Conflict
filmstrip/color/record or cassette/Teacher's Guide/Center for the Humanities
    The program suggests that hostility and aggression may not be instinctive,
    but learned cultural values. In society today, we happen to value the
    successful business person and professional athlete more than the
    non-competitive individual.

Man and His Values: An Inquiry into Good and Evil
filmstrip/color/record or cassette/Teacher's Guide/Center for the Humanities
    Examines the innate duality of our nature and traces historically the
    various concepts of good and evil constructed by society, religion and the
    state.

<u>The Man in the Glass Booth</u>
117 minutes/color/Films, Inc.
    An excellent feature film with Maximilian Schell about a man obsessed with
    finding responsibility for what happened to Jews in the Holocaust.

<u>Manzanar</u>
15 minutes/Visual Communications
    A man's recollections of his life at Manzanar, the Japanese relocation camp,
    when he was a small boy.

<u>Martin Luther King, Jr.: From Montgomery to Memphis</u>
27 minutes/black and white/ADL
    This film follows the career of Martin Luther King, Jr., from the early bus
    boycott in 1956 to his tragic assassination in 1968. Very well done.

<u>The Martyr</u>
90 minutes/color/Joseph Green Pictures
    Feature film based on the story of Dr. Janus Korczak's valiant efforts to
    help orphaned children in the Warsaw Ghetto.

<u>A Matter of Conscience</u>
30 minutes/color/Learning Corporation of America
    A film about the difficult ethical decision made by Sir Thomas More when he
    refused to sanction one of the marriages of Henry VIII.

<u>Mein Kampf</u>
119 minutes/black and white/Films, Inc.
    A documentary depiction of the rise of Hitler and the Third Reich.

<u>Memorandum</u>
58 minutes/black and white/ADL
    Twenty years after their liberation, a group of survivors return to
    Germany. This documentary compares the Germany of the Third Reich with the
    Germany of the present.

<u>Memorial</u>
17 minutes/color/ADL
    The heroic efforts of those German clergy, labor leaders, and students who
    fought against the Nazis are documented in this film. Most perished for
    their bravery.

<u>Metropolis</u>
133 minutes/black and white/Museum of Modern Art
    Fritz Lang's vision of a future society done in Germany in the late 1920's.

<u>Monkeys, Apes and Man</u>
52 minutes/color/Films, Inc.
    A well-done exploration of primate behavior and similarities between
    primates and humans. Discusses the work of Harry Haarlow and Desmond
    Morris.

<u>Moral Development</u>
25 minutes/color/CRM—McGraw Hill
    Recreates Stanley Milgram's famous "shock" experiment while implementing the
    pioneering "moral stages" of Dr. Lawrence Kohlberg.

The Music of Auschwitz
16 minutes/color/ADL
     Made for "60 Minutes," this segment tells the story of Fania Fenalon, the
     French Jewish musician, who was sent to a concentration camp.

My Country, Right or Wrong
15 minutes/color/Learning Corporation of America
     A film about a man who does not want to fight in Vietnam but who has a
     father who demands he fulfill his "obligation" to his country.

Nazi Holocaust Series I
Twenty-five 11" x 14" photo aids/Teacher's Guide/Social Studies School Service
     Documentary.

Nazi Holocaust Series II
Forty 11" x 14" photo aids/Teacher's Guide/Social Studies School Service
     Documentary.

Nazi War Criminals in the U.S.
     An ABC television documentary about alleged Nazis living in the U.S.

Night and Fog
31 minutes/color/ADL
     In this unique film, cameras are taken to major concentration camps, now
     hauntingly barren, and over these scenes is superimposed historic footage
     evoking the dreadful past. French narration with English subtitles.

Nightmare: The Immigration of Joachim and Rachel
24 minutes/color/Multimedia
     Two children struggling to escape from the Warsaw Ghetto. A dramatic
     reenactment. For junior high level.

Nisei: The Pride and the Shame
30 minutes/black and white/Association Films
     Originally part of the CBS-TV "20th Century" series. Narrated by Walter
     Cronkite, the film presents an overview of the evacuation experience.

One Man
30 minutes/Films, Inc.
     This film portrays the case of Raoul Wallenberg, the Swedish diplomat who
     disappeared while attempting to save the Jews of Hungary.

The Pawnbroker
116 minutes/black and white/Films, Inc.
     This feature film offers a portrait of a man who survived a Nazi
     concentration camp only to encounter further horrors in Harlem.

The Prejudice Film
28 minutes/color/Motivational Media
     David Hartman narrates this exploration into the different kinds of
     prejudice and how they are expressed.

Pressure Point
89 minutes/black and white/United Artists
> A feature film with Sidney Poitier and Bobby Darin about understanding an American Nazi in a prison camp during World War II. An excellent portrayal of a Nazi personality.

The Psychology of Man: An Inquiry into Human Behavior
slides/sound/Center for the Humanities
> Outlines the various approaches to the study of human behavior.

Puppets
11 minutes/black and white/ADL
> A puppet actor steps out of his role in a marionette performance of "Julius Caeser" to provide a unique lesson on totalitarianism and conformity.

OB VII
video cassette/Columbia Pictures Home Entertainment
> Based on the novel by Leon Uris, the television production starring Ben Gazzara faithfully tells the story of a Christian doctor who collaborated with the Nazis in a concentration camp.

Relocation of Japanese-Americans
2 filmstrips/black and white/cassettes/Teacher's Guide/Zenger Productions
> The first filmstrip gives the historical background to the relocation of the Japanese-Americans during World War II. The second deals with the actual wartime evacuation.

The Rise and Fall of Nazi Germany
Part I: Rise of Hitler
28 minutes/black and white/ADL/also 3/4" video cassette
> The film chronicles how Adolf Hitler and his political cohorts in the Nazi party manipulated events during their country's crises to achieve power: their promulgation of the myth of the Aryan race gave Germans an outlet for their hate and frustrations; the Nazis forced a political crisis to overthrow the democratic Weimar Republic; and Hitler emerged as the Chancellor of the Third Reich.

Part II: Nazi Germany: Years of Triumph
28 minutes/black and white/ADL/also 3/4" video cassette
> Germany between 1933 and 1939 when some 67 million people willingly became puppets of the Third Reich. There was little resistance to Hitler's conquests in Eastern Europe until he invaded Poland. Finally, the Allies resisted.

Part III: Gotterdammerung: Collapse of the Third Reich
28 minutes/black and white/ADL/also 3/4" video cassette
> In the four years between 1941 and 1945, Hitler's dream of a "thousand year Reich" turned into the nightmare of World War II as the free nations of the world joined together to defeat Nazi tyranny.

Part IV: Nuremberg Trial
31 minutes/black and white/ADL/also 3/4" video cassette
> The indictment of 24 Nazi leaders in Nuremberg, Germany, in October, 1945, opened an unprecedented chapter in international law.

The Roots of Adolf Hitler's Mind
filmstrips/record or cassette/Social Studies School Service
> Based on a secret wartime psychological study, this two-part filmstrip
> examines the factors which led Hitler to become the most infamous of
> dictators.

Sacco and Vanzetti
118 minutes/color/dubbed/Films, Inc.
> This film is a searing account of the infamous 1920 trial in which two
> Italian immigrants struggled to clear themselves of a murder/robbery charge.

Seeds of Hate
2 filmstrips/records or cassettes/Clearview
> Investigates the origins of prejudice and how they are expressed.

Self-Standing Exhibit on the Holocaust
> Thirty-three panels of photos and charts available on loan. Shipping
> charges. American Federation of Jewish Fighters, Camp Inmates/Nazi Victims.

Seven Beauties
116 minutes/color/subtitles/Cinema Guild
> The controversial movie by Lina Wertmuller about one man's experience in
> wartime Italy. Contains scenes supposedly depicting life at Auschwitz.
> Much discussion about the film concerns the willingness of the central
> character to do anything to survive.

Ship of Fools
150 minutes/black and white/Films, Inc.
> A German passenger freighter is sailing from Mexico to Bremen in 1933. This
> feature film traces with insight, irony and humor a variety of situations
> and characters in a powerful and compelling study of humanity in the world
> that gave rise to Hitler.

The Shop on Main Street
128 minutes/black and white/Mass Media Ministries and Films, Inc.
> A moving film about an elderly Jewish woman and a young Czech man's
> reactions to her plight when the Nazis round up the Jews in Czechoslovakia.
> Based on the novel by Ladislaw Grossman.

Silences
12 minutes/color/CRM-McGraw Hill
> A film about a Yugoslavian civilian during the war who tries to save the
> life of the enemy, one German soldier. A disturbing conclusion.

Starpower: Simulation
Grade Level: 10-Adult/Subject Area: Political Science/Number of Players: 18-40
Western Behavioral Sciences Institute

Swastika
Simulation/Social Studies School Service
> Students assume the roles of Jews, German citizens, and S.S. troops. They
> must determine which of the civilians are Jews and imprison them. Christian
> civilians must decide whether to aid the Jews or merely stay out of
> trouble. The game requires more than one coordinator and more than one
> classroom. Players: 20-40. Time: 3 hours or 3 class periods.

<u>The Sioux: As Long as the Grass Grows and the Water Flows</u>
filmstrip/color/record or cassette/script/Social Studies School Service
    Using the Sioux as a case study, this filmstrip examines the conflicts that
    destroyed Native American culture.

<u>The Sixties</u>
black and white/Pyramid
    Charles Braverman's excellent film which briefly shows the spirit of that
    controversial decade through some very graphic film excerpts.

<u>The Twisted Cross</u>
54 minutes/black and white/CRM-McGraw Hill
    A classic documentary depicting the rise and fall of Nazism. Originally an
    NBC television production.

<u>To See or Not To See</u>
15 minutes/color/Learning Corporation of America
    A short film with a "psychological" point of view about a doctor who
    recommends that people wear glasses so that they don't see reality as it
    truly is. Deals with the need for illusion.

<u>Triumph of the Will</u>
120 minutes/also 50-minute version/black and white/German without subtitles/CRM-
McGraw Hill or Images/Beta or VHS video cassettes/110-minutes/Teacher's Guide/
Social Studies School Service
    Infamous powerful propaganda film by Leni Riefenstahl of the 1934 Nazi Party
    rally in Nuremberg.

<u>Understanding Prejudice</u>
filmstrips/color/records or cassettes/available individually/Sunburst
Communications or ADL
    <u>Stereotyping and Generalizing</u>: Defines prejudice, shows its relation to
    stereotyping; explains how stereotyping differs from valid generalizing.
    Describes the nature of prejudice -- how it is formed and how it may be
    altered.
    <u>Master Race Myth</u>: Emphasizes the fact that there is no relation between
    intelligence and physical appearance, that all people really are similar,
    and that differences are mainly due to varied environments.
    <u>Scapegoating</u>: Explores what scapegoating is; how it differs from
    discrimination; examines scapegoating through three case studies.

<u>Values - What Young People Choose To Live and Die for: Case Studies in Conflict</u>
filmstrip/sound/color/Teacher's Guide/Center for the Humanities
    Four historical incidents are dramatized in terms of conflicting values.
    Students are asked to define those values, formulate opinions on why the
    conflicts occurred and explore parallels in contemporary history.

<u>Verdict for Tomorrow</u>
28 minutes/black and white/ADL
    An account of the Eichmann trial, narrated by Lowell Thomas.

Violence in America: John Brown
Multi Media Education
     A filmstrip which raises the issue of whether John Brown's violent actions
     against slavery were ethically justifiable.

Violence Just for Fun
14 minutes/color/Learning Corporation of America
     Taken from "Barabbas," this well-done film explores the world of the
     gladiator and the arena, and what they reveal about human behavior.

Voyage of the Damned
158 minutes/color/Swank
     The story of the 937 German-Jewish refugees aboard S.S. St. Louis who sailed
     to Cuba in 1939 but were forced to return to Europe.

War Crimes
filmstrip/cassette/Teacher's Guide/Zenger
     Through the study and comparison of the war crimes and trials of German and
     Japanese leaders after World War II and the crimes in Vietnam, including the
     trial of Lt. Calley, students learn that there are no simple answers to
     questions of morality.

The Warsaw Ghetto
filmstrip/130 frames/cassette/Jewish Labor Committee
     Theodore Bikel narrates the story of Jewish resistance against Nazi might
     that stayed the German war machine for 42 days.

Warsaw Ghetto
51 minutes/black and white/ADL
     Footage taken from 1940 to 1943 of the Warsaw Ghetto. Pictures of life and
     death in the ghetto were taken by camermen of the German Army, the S.S. and
     Gestapo. Produced by BBC-TV.

The Weimar Republic: Germany from Democracy to Hitler
2 filmstrips/cassette/Teacher's Guide/Listening Library
     Beginning in pre-war Germany, this filmstrip set carefully traces the
     fateful path from plutocratic monarchy to democratic republic to
     totalitarian dictatorship.

What Does It Mean To Be Human?
slides/color/Teacher's Guide/Center for the Humanities
     Opening with a quote from Carl Sandburg's "Wilderness," part one focuses on
     the coordination of the brain and hand, which gives us dexterity, and that
     of the brain and vocal organs, which makes speech possible. Part two
     explains that humans are by nature social, and that their societies share
     certain basic characteristics. Part three explores civilization as a
     distinctly human invention and shows how civilized societies are
     differentiated from folk or tribal societies.

Whether to Tell the Truth
18 minutes/color/Learning Corporation of America
     Taken from the Academy Award winning film, "On the Waterfront," this raises
     the issue of whether one man should tell the truth and thus face possible
     reprisal. Starring Marlon Brando.

ABC-TV
1330 Ave. of the Americas
New York, N.Y.

Alden Films
7820 - 20th Avenue
Brooklyn, N.Y. 11214

American Federation of Jewish Fighters,
    Camp Inmates and Nazi Victims
505 Fifth Avenue
New York, N.Y. 10017

Anti-Defamation League of B'nai B'rith
823 United Nations Plaza
New York, N.Y. 10017

Association Films
866 Third Avenue
New York, N.Y.

Atlantis Films
1252 La Granda Dr.
Thousand Oaks, CA 91360

Audio Visual Narrative Arts
29 Marble Ave.
Pleasantville, N.Y. 10570

Center for the Humanities, Inc.
2 Holland Avenue
White Plains, N.Y. 10603

Center for Mass Communications
Columbia University Press
562 West 113 Street
New York, N.Y. 10025

Cinema 5
1500 Broadway
New York, N.Y. 10036

Cinema Guild
1697 Broadway
New York, N.Y. 10019

Clearview
5711 N. Milwaukee Ave.
Chicago, IL. 60646

Columbia Pictures Home Entertainment
711 Fifth Avenue
New York, N.Y.

CRM/McGraw Hill Films
P.O.B. 641
Del Mar, CA 92014

Educational Audio-Visual, Inc.
17 Marble Avenue
Pleasantville, N.Y. 10570

Encylopaedia Britannica Films
310 S. Michigan
Chicago, IL. 60604

Film Wright
4530 - 18th Street
San Francisco, CA. 94114

Films, Inc.
733 Green Bay Rd.
Wilmette, IL. 60091

Franciscan Communications Center
1229 Sands Santee
Los Angeles, CA. 90015

Joseph Green Pictures
200 West 58 Street
New York, N.Y. 10019

Indiana University Film Library
Bloomington, IN. 47405

Janus Films
119 West 57 Street
New York, N.Y. 10019

Jewish Labor Committee
25 East 78 Street
New York, N.Y. 10021

Jewish Media Center
15 East 26 Street
New York, N.Y. 10010

Learning Corporation of America
1750 Avenue of the Americas
New York, N.Y.

Listening Library, Inc.
One Park Avenue
Old Greenwich, CT. 06870

Mass Media Associates
1720 Chateau
St. Louis, MO. 63103

Mass Media Ministry
2116 N. Charles Street
Baltimore, MD. 21218

Motivational Media, Inc.
6855 Santa Monica Blvcd., Suite#404
Los Angeles, CA. 90038

Multimedia
140 West 9 Street
Cincinnati, OH. 45202

Museum of Modern Art
11 West 53 Street
New York, N.Y. 10020

National Academy for Adult Jewish Studies
155 Fifth Avenue
New York, N. Y. 10010

PBS
609 Fifth Avenue
New York, N.Y.

Pyramid Films
P.O.B. 1048
Santa Monica, CA. 90406

Scholastic
50 West 44 Street
New York, N.Y. 10036

Social Studies School Service
10,000 Culver Blvd.
Culver City, CA. 90230

Sunburst Communications
39 Washington Avenue
Pleasantville, N.Y. 10570

Swank
201 S. Jefferson Avenue
St. Louis, M.O. 63116

United Artists 16
729 Seventh Avenue
New York, N.Y. 10019

Universal Pictures
445 Park Avenue
New York, N.Y.

Visual Communications
313 South San Pedro Street
Los Angeles, CA. 90013

Western Behavioral Sciences
  Institute (WBSCI)
1150 Silverade Street
La Jolla, CA. 92037

Clem Williams
2240 Noblestown Road
Pittsburgh. PA. 15205

Zenger Productions, Inc.
Documentary Photo Aids
Box 802
Culver City, CA. 90230

<u>18% Call Nazi Era The Good Old Days</u>

Associated Press

BONN, Germany -- A public opinion poll has found that 18 percent of West German voters look back on the era of Nazi dictator Adolf Hitler as "the good old days," a leading magazine reported yesterday.

The magazine Der Spiegel said a year-long, government-ordered survey by the Sinus Institute of Munich found that 18 percent of the 6,968 voters questioned nationwide agreed that "under Hitler, Germany really had it better."

Der Spiegel claimed that the findings so alarmed the office of Chancellor Helmut Schmidt that they have been kept under wraps since the survey was completed last year.

A government spokesman confirmed that the chancellor's office had requested the survey to determine the extent of rightist sentiment within West Germany.

The spokesman, who asked not to be identified, said he had read the Spiegel report and found it correct.

In addition to those sympathetic with Hitler's rule, the survey reportedly found that despite a generation of democracy, a sizable number of West Germans support many of the fundamental doctrines of Nazism.

Most of the potential Nazis are more than 50 years old, the magazine said. That would make them old enough to remember Hitler, who ruled Germany from 1933 until his suicide in the ruins of Berlin in 1945.

"A total of 13 percent of the voters [about 5.5 million] have an ideologically closed, extreme rightist world view, the main supports of which are a National Socialist view of history, hatred of foreigners, democracy and pluralism, and an exaggerated devotion to people, fatherland and family," the magazine said.

"Almost half of these extreme rightists, that is about 6 percent of the eligible voters, accept politically motivated force, up to and including terror against people.

"Unprecedentedly, many rightist radicals come from villages of between 2,000 and 5,000 inhabitants, from small town and from rural areas around big cities," the magazine quoted the survey as finding.

Most of them also live in the federal states of Bavaria and Hesse in southern Germany, the magazine said.

The survey also reportedly found that 37 percent of those surveyed rejected Nazism, militarism and the "fuhrer cult" but were "authoritatively disposed."

Der Spiegel said the survey found among rightists widespread resentment against the United States, which they felt had forced West Germany to abandon traditional virtues for a culture of "Coca-Cola imperialism, beat and drug culture, disco, Hollywood and jeans."

The West German government has expressed increasing alarm during the last three years over the increase in the number of radical rightist and neo-Nazi groups.

Rightists were believed behind the slaying last August of a Vietnamese refugee in Hamburg and the explosion last September at Munich's Oktoberfest beer festival which claimed 13 lives.

March 17, 1981

'Holocaust' Stirs Memories of Switzerland's Epoch of Guilt
By Hanns Neuerbourg

ZURICH, Switzerland -- "Holocaust," the U.S. televison series on the World War II German massacre of Jews, came up on Swiss television screens last week, stirring bitter reminders that neutral Switzerland's wartime record has an "ugly spot," as a prominent Swiss historian calls it.

It is a little-publicized fact that Swiss authorities, fearing German reprisals, sent back to Nazi control thousands of Jewish refugees who had managed to flee into Switzerland or were stopped by Swiss border guards.

Swiss researchers have long said that the official policy, contradicting the country's humanitarian traditions, meant a virtual death sentence for those who were refused shelter. But not before the screening of "Holocaust" has such a broad audience been confronted with this chapter of Swiss history.

"Watching 'Holocaust,' the postwar generation asks also about our own past," the newspaper Basler Zeitung commented. The answers have come in dozens of articles, radio commentaries and TV discussions.

Blick, Switzerland's top-circulation tabloid, published a 10,000-word series titled "The Swiss Holocaust."

Writing in the conservative Neue Zuercher Zeitung, a young historian, Georg Kreis, recalled that Switzerland, after admitting thousands of exiles during the early years of Adolf Hitler's Third Reich, tightened its policies in 1938. Swiss authorities, he wrote, proposed then that the Germans stamp passports of German "non-Aryans" with a "J" for Jew to facilitate Swiss border controls.

Swiss postwar research, which has resurfaced with the showing of "Holocaust," indicated a growing awareness of Switzerland's island-like position in the middle of Axis-controlled Europe made the government decide in 1942 to take radical action. Even the United States' entry into the war had failed to shake some leading Swiss -- including the foreign minister of the time, Marcel Pilet -- in their conviction that Hitler would eventually win.

According to researchers, the government's police issued orders in August 1942 that refugees fleeing to Switzerland "only for racial reasons" were to be turned back. French Jews, the orders specified, should be sent back "without exception" on the grounds that they were "not exposed to danger" in their Nazi-occupied country. In one week alone that autumn, more than 2,200 refugees were returned to German control.

Border guards witnessed shocking scenes. "Often people killed themselves in front of the Swiss soldiers so they would not fall into the hands of the Germans," said an official Swiss report.

"The winter of 1942-43 and the summer of 1943 has gone down in Swiss history...as dark epochs," Professor Edgar Bonjour wrote in his "History of Swiss Neutrality" in 1970.

"The amount of human despair compressed in these months is still burdening the conscience of the people," he said.

Press comments last week on "Holocaust" concur that the government had ample information about the Nazi extermination machinery even before it virtually sealed its borders in 1942.

"The non-occupied European states which continued to turn away the Jews ... even when there was no longer the slightest doubt about their fate thus became accomplices of the mass murderers," commented the Zurich weekly newspaper Weltwoche.

A Swiss radio commentator said some members of the all-Swiss International Committee of the Red Cross had proposed in 1942 a public appeal by the Red Cross to draw attention to the fate of the Jews. But a majority on the committee prevented publication of even a vague statement that "mentioned neither the Third Reich nor the concentration camps nor the Jews," the commentary said.

It added Red Cross officials apparently feared the Germans would react to such an appeal by closing prisoner-of-war camps to visits by Red Cross delegates, a right laid down in the Geneva conventions.

"Apparently, they asked themselves whether the saving of people who were not very liked was worth such a risk," the commentator said.

As the Allies advanced, Swiss authorities relaxed their curbs. Thousands of Jews were admitted into Switzerland again, especially in the late summer of 1943 when the German SS was reported to be searching northern Italy for new victims of the "final solution."

At the end of the war, more than 115,000 refugees were in Switzerland, 10 times the number three years earlier. Swiss individuals and private charity organizations gave them generous help.

Still, Bonjour wrote in 1970, "an ugly spot on the Swiss shield of Swiss neutrality remains."

"A whole generation failed and shares the guilt," he added. "The egotist and the latent anti-Semite in every citizen made him close his eyes to certain inhumane aspects of official policy.

"Courageous people ... stood up and protested openly. But they were not able to stir the silent majority -- which perhaps felt likewise -- out of its indolence."

May 13, 1979

<u>Holocaust Was Hard To Believe: So They Died</u>

By Garry Wills

In a sense, there is nothing new to say about the Holocaust. But in another (and even more important) sense, there is everything to say, since we must always start over with this indigestible bit of our recent history - it is so horrible that we must convince ourselves, each time we reconsider it, that it really did happen.

We are always starting again on it because it takes us back to the most basic issues of evil, ignorance and the human condition. Our inability to understand the Holocaust begins then, with the simple difficulty of believing in it.

Walter Laqueur has now published a study, in the current issue of Encounter magazine, of the way this rejection of the facts worked on the people who first received reports of the Holocaust.

All through 1942, the evidence accumulated that as many as a million Jews had been murdered. But this news was reported sporadically, perfunctorily, in ways that subtly downplayed not only the horror but the reality of the reports.

Laqueur, whose article is an extract from a forthcoming book, soberly considers the motives for this rejection. Was there a conspiracy to hide the facts? Not quite -- though there was an informal agreement by Allied propagandists that emphasis on the Jews' plight would not aid the war effort. Why was that?

Partly, of course, because of the anti-Semitism still widespread among the Allied powers. Partly from the sense the Jews were exaggerating.

But Laqueur sees a deeper reason behind all these partial rationalizations. Some of those who rejected or neglected the evidence were clearly not anti-Semitic. Not only did Franklin Roosevelt treat the evidence skeptically, at times flippantly, so did Justic Felix Frankfurter tend to block it out.

Our ability to reject unwelcome facts is one of the most interesting -- and, often, disheartening - facts about humankind. I have often said, and sometimes written, that the old Candid Camera show was a cruel but instructive course of psychology.

When Allen Funt sprang contrived miracles on unsuspecting people, they did not argue with the unexpected, or actively disbelieve, in most cases. They just ignored the inconvenient event. What cannot be understood will not even be noticed.

It makes me wonder -- what victims are we ignoring now? Boat people? The unborn?

For years we hid from ourselves the tyranny exercised over our own black
fellow citizens. (F.D.R. worked in the '30s to block anti-lynching planks in
the Democratic platforms.) Even if we descend, or ascend, from the horror of
multiple lives taken, what rights denied do we deny the reality of? Those of
Palestinians? Of gay people?

It shook many people years ago, that a woman could be killed at leisure in
New York's streets while dozens of people systematically closed their ears to
her screaming. The evidence is that at times we all tune out the cries of entire
multitudes. Which is another reason why we hate to study the Holocaust, and the
best reason why we have to.

August 6, 1980

Student Anthology

Table of Contents

About the Editors

Richard F. Flaim

Mr. Richard F. Flaim is presently Supervisor of Social Studies, K-12, for the Vineland (N.J.) Public Schools and previously served the district as Social Studies Department Chairperson and teacher at Vineland High School. Mr. Flaim is a doctoral candidate in Educational Administration and Supervision at Rutgers University. He is past-President of the New Jersey Council for the Social Studies, a member of the N.J. Advisory Council on Holocaust Education, and the NCSS Advisory Committee on Racism and Social Justice. He has been a consultant and co-director for the New Jersey State Department of Education Holocaust Education Project.

Edwin W. Reynolds

Mr. Edwin W. Reynolds received his BA and MAT degrees from Fairleigh Dickinson University, and is presently the Social Studies Supervisor, K-12, for the Teaneck (N.J.) Public Schools. He is a member of the Board of Directors of the National Council for the Social Studies and past-President of the National Social Studies Supervisors Association. Mr. Reynolds is a member of the N.J. Advisory Council on Holocaust Education and serves as co-director and consultant to the N.J. Holocaust Education Project at the State Department of Education.

John W. Chupak

Mr. John Chupak received his BA and MA degrees from Jersey City State College, and is presently a social studies teacher at Teaneck (N.J.) High School. He is a past member of the Board of Directors of the New Jersey Council for the Social Studies, and a former commissioner with the Clifton Historical Commission. He co-authored a learning guide about the Holocaust for the Anti-Defamation League and is a consultant for the New Jersey State Department of Education Holocaust Eduation Project.

Harry Furman

Mr. Harry Furman is a teacher of American Social and Political Behavior and The Conscience of Man at Vineland (N.J.) High School. He is a doctoral candidate in American History at Rutgers University, and is concurrently pursuing a law degree at Rutgers. He is a child of survivors, and has played a prominent role in the development of awareness and interest in teaching about the Holocaust. He has conducted numerous teacher-training seminars and has spoken at conferences on the Holocaust and genocide, nationwide. He is a consultant to the New Jersey State Department of Education and to local school districts on Holocaust Education.

Kenneth Tubertini

Mr. Kenneth Tubertini received his BS in History from Rider College and his MA in American History from Temple University. At present he is a teacher of Honors American History and American Social and Political Behavior at Vineland (N.J.) High School. He has served as consultant to local school districts and the New Jersey State Department of Education and has conducted regional and national workshops on Holocaust Education.

ANTI-DEFAMATION LEAGUE OF B'NAI B'RITH
823 United Nations Plaza, New York, NY 10017 _______________ (212) 490-2525

REGIONAL OFFICES
ARIZONA REGIONAL OFFICE
The First Interstate Tower, 3550 North Central Ave., Suite 1520, Phoenix, AZ 85012 (602) 274-0991
CENTRAL PACIFIC REGIONAL OFFICE
760 Market Street, Suite 837, San Francisco, CA 94102 _______________ (415) 391-0200
CONNECTICUT REGIONAL OFFICE
1162 Chapel Street, New Haven, CT 06511 _______________ (203) 787-4281
D.C.-MARYLAND REGIONAL OFFICE
1640 Rhode Island Avenue, N.W., Washington, DC 20036 _______________ (202) 857-6660
EASTERN PENNSYLVANIA/DELAWARE
225 South 15th St., Philadelphia, PA 19102 _______________ (215) 735-4267
FLORIDA REGIONAL OFFICE
150 SE 2nd Avenue, Suite 800, Miami, FL 33131 _______________ (305) 373-6306
JEWISH COMMUNITY RELATIONS COUNCIL, ANTI-DEFAMATION
LEAGUE OF MINNESOTA AND THE DAKOTAS
15 South 9th Street, Minneapolis, MN 55402 _______________ (612) 338-7816
LONG ISLAND REGIONAL OFFICE
98 Cutter Mill Rd., Great Neck, NY 11021 _______________ (516) 829-3820
MICHIGAN REGIONAL OFFICE
163 Madison Avenue, Suite 120, Detroit, MI 48226 _______________ (313) 962-9686
MIDWEST REGIONAL OFFICE
222 West Adams Street, Chicago, IL 60606 _______________ (312) 782-5080
MISSOURI-SOUTHERN ILLINOIS REGIONAL OFFICE
225 S. Meramec, Clayton, MO 63105 _______________ (314) 726-3303
MOUNTAIN STATES REGIONAL OFFICE
300 South Dahlia Street, Suite 202, Denver, CO 80222 _______________ (303) 321-7177
NEW ENGLAND REGIONAL OFFICE
72 Franklin Street, Suite 504, Boston, MA 02110 _______________ (617) 542-4977
NEW JERSEY REGIONAL OFFICE
513 West Mt. Pleasant Avenue, Livingston, NJ 07039 _______________ (201) 994-4546
NEW YORK CITY REGIONAL OFFICE
823 United Nations Plaza, New York, NY 10017 _______________ (212) 490-2525
NEW YORK STATE REGIONAL OFFICE
65 South Broadway, Tarrytown, NY 10591 _______________ (914) 332-1166
NORTH CAROLINA-VIRGINIA REGIONAL OFFICE
3311 West Broad Street, Richmond, VA 23230 _______________ (804) 355-2884
NORTHWEST TEXAS-OKLAHOMA REGIONAL OFFICE
12800 Hillcrest Rd., Suite 219, Dallas, TX 75230 _______________ (214) 960-0342
OHIO-KENTUCKY-INDIANA REGIONAL OFFICE
1175 College Avenue, Columbus, OH 43209 _______________ (614) 239-8414
ORANGE COUNTY REGIONAL OFFICE
2700 North Main Street, Suite 500, Santa Ana, CA 92701 _______________ (714) 973-4733
PACIFIC NORTHWEST REGIONAL OFFICE
1809 7th Avenue, Suite 1609, Seattle, WA 98101 _______________ (206) 624-5750
PACIFIC SOUTHWEST REGIONAL OFFICE
6505 Wilshire Boulevard, Suite 814, Los Angeles, CA 90048 _______________ (213) 655-8205
PALM BEACH COUNTY REGIONAL OFFICE
120 So. Olive Avenue, Suite 400, West Palm Beach, FL 33401 _______________ (305) 832-7144
PLAINS STATES REGIONAL OFFICE
333 So. 132 Street, Omaha, NB 68154 _______________ (402) 333-1303
SAN DIEGO REGIONAL OFFICE
7850 Mission Center Court #207, San Diego, CA 92108 _______________ (619) 293-3770
SOUTH CENTRAL REGIONAL OFFICE
535 Gravier Street, Suite 501, New Orleans, LA 70130 _______________ (504) 522-9534
SOUTHEAST REGIONAL OFFICE
805 Peachtree Street, NE, Suite 633, Atlanta, GA 30308 _______________ (404) 523-3391
SOUTHWEST REGIONAL OFFICE
4211 Southwest Freeway, Suite 209, Houston, TX 77027 _______________ (713) 627-3490
WESTERN PENNSYLVANIA/WEST VIRGINIA REGIONAL OFFICE
Allegheny Bldg., 429 Forbes St., 7th Fl., Pittsburgh, PA 15219 _______________ (412) 471-1050

ABROAD
ISRAEL OFFICE
30 King David Street, Jerusalem _______________ (02) 224-844
PARIS OFFICE
Boite Postale No. 17-75261, Paris, CEDEX 06, France _______________ (01) 222-12-02
ROME LIAISON OFFICE
Via San Crescenziano 11, 00199, Rome, Italy _______________ (06) 831-0761